W9-DBW-511

YOUNG PEOPLE IN COMMUNAL LIVING

YOUNG PEOPLE
IN
COMMUNAL
LIVING
by DENHAM GRIERSON

W

THE WESTMINSTER PRESS
Philadelphia

PUBLISHED BY THE WESTMINSTER PRESS ®
PHILADELPHIA, PENNSYLVANIA

PRINTED IN THE UNITED STATES OF AMERICA

TO MAVIS

FOREWORD

IN OCTOBER OF 1968 a task force composed of young adults, clergy on the cutting edge of the church, and some very open laymen began to shape a vision. The vision was of a Community of young adults spending a year together preparing to participate in the urban revolution. For nine months this task force struggled to shape the model for such a year. Finally, in the spring of 1969 their tentative product was submitted to experts in the fields of theology, group process, and urban ministry. This further refined product was then brought into the sunlight of reality.

A Community of young adults was assembled who committed themselves to a year together. Denham Grierson was selected to be reflector to the group. The pages that follow are a record of that year in the sunlight and an interpretation of the happening. Our hope is that others may find our journey useful.

JAMES REID
Dean of the Northside Lay Academy

CONTENTS

And you wait, awaiting the one
to make your small life grow:
the mighty, the uncommon,
the awakening of stone,
the depths to be opened below.

. . . .

And suddenly know: It was here!
You pull yourself together and there
stands an irrevocable year
of anguish and vision and prayer.

—*From "Memory,"*
       by Rainer Maria Rilke.

Originally published by the University of
California Press; reprinted by permission
of The Regents of the University of
California.

YOUNG PEOPLE IN COMMUNAL LIVING

I

YOUTH IN COMMUNITY:
THE SEARCH FOR VISION

A STRANGE HOUSE. A new beginning. The living room a
jumble of furniture, trunks, and bodies. An air about the
place vaguely like the first day at a new school. A sweet
smell in the air—Incense? Ashtrays all around. Several
unlighted candles. A rattle of coffee cups from the
kitchen. The only available space a third of a mattress
in one corner of the room. An odd assortment of travelers
indeed. It seemed a long time before everyone was settled and the small talk abated. The meeting began.

The occasion was the first gathering of a group of
young people, most of them strangers to each other as
well as to me, who were to spend a year of their lives
together. All of us had expectations, hopes, and limita-
tions completely hidden behind a charming friendliness
that at one and the same time kept us in touch and also
at bay. There was an atmosphere of excitement, a sense
of watching and waiting, and a faith that we could forge
some kind of future together. If it is true that young
people in American society are on a journey in search
of themselves, then that night we set out on a voyage of
self-discovery. What follows is the chronicle of an odys-

sey, the story of what took place and a little of what we learned together.

This first meeting occurred in the latter part of September of 1969, the initial gathering of the Community for Urban Encounter, a project sponsored by the Chicago Northside Lay Academy. The Academy received its principal support and funding from the Northern Illinois Conference of The United Methodist Church and the Methodist Volunteer Organization. Those who applied for admittance to the program committed themselves to living in Community for a year. Participants worked during the day in jobs in the city of Chicago in order to support themselves.

Most of the Community members lived in the same quarters, a house rented for the duration of the Community's life. It was here that all subsequent meetings were held and the Community lived out its existence. As one of the Community members said, "Tell those who read the story to read slowly and thoughtfully." Perhaps he is right. The truth lies between the lines as much as in them.

THE BEGINNING

How were the members recruited? What did they have in common? Did they share a common understanding of the project?

The simplest of these to answer is the question about recruitment. No rigorous criteria for selection were used. Some members were contacted through summer programs run by the Academy; some were contacted personally, and, in coming, brought their friends; others were directed to the venture by the Methodist Volunteer Organization. Some were natives of Chicago. Others came from hundreds of miles from Chicago. When the Community was able to stand up and count its members, there were fourteen in all, including two staff members of the Northside Lay Academy.

In the following pages the term "Community" refers to this particular group. It does not represent a goal that members were seeking. For our purposes, "Community" always designates the group and its intentions.

What did this disparate group of young people have in common? The answer is: very little. The age range was from twenty-nine to eighteen, with an average in the low twenties. A questionnaire completed by nine members in the first phase of the Community's life substantiates this claim. Questions called for an attitudinal response rated on a 1 to 10 basis, 1 representing strongest disagreement, 10 strongest agreement. Topics ranged over Mayor Daley's handling of the Democratic Convention disorders, actions of the SDS, the Kerner Report, the Black Power movement, civil rights, the welfare system, political existence, military duty, and the role of the church in social affairs. Only on one question was there any substantial agreement. In response to the statement, "Every American male should be a patriotic citizen and serve his country by performing his required military duty," eight scored 1, one person scored 4. What the questionnaire did reveal, however, was what appeared at first to be a surprising conservatism on most issues. Members were more unanimously against things in general than for anything in particular.

A large percentage of the group were college dropouts.

One was still in college. Others had their degrees and were looking for jobs. Some were mild drug users. Others were strongly opposed to drugs. Several were engaged in alternative service in hospitals as conscientious objectors. Other members, although opposed to the war, were willing to be drafted if it could not be avoided. There was a sharp division concerning sexual behavior. Several were politically conservative. Others were close to the far left.

A few members saw themselves as belonging to the counterculture symbolized by the hippie movement. Others expected to make their way in the present system. The distribution of the sexes was roughly equivalent. Some members came from rich homes, some from poor; some from large families, some from small.

Three of the members were children of clergymen; others, at best, had only a tangential relationship to the church. Only a few were regular in attendance at worship, and some had not been to church in recent memory. One of the group, who played the electric guitar (loudly), was a devotee of rock. Others preferred folk music. In short, a more diverse group of people could hardly have been gathered, even if a deliberate effort had been made to do so.

Yet, despite this diversity, there was a unity that bound the group together, nonetheless real because it could not easily be put into words. The elements of this unity included a feeling of alienation in the present society, a sense of dislocation in that there was no place where the members were really at home. Even more fundamental was the search for a job worth doing that might liberate them from the sense that it didn't much matter what you did, given what seemed to them the irreversible direction of the culture in which they lived. Behind the quest for communal experience, members shared a search for a unifying vision that would mobilize their energies, invest life with meaning, and offer them a usable future in which they might truly find themselves. This mutuality of concern was not at first apparent.

Did they share a common understanding of the project? The initial situation was even more confused because members were as devoid of a common mind concerning the purpose of the Community as they were about most everything else. The question, "What are you looking for in the Community for Urban Encounter?" elicited from the nine people the following diffuse and varied responses:

Involvement and better understanding of the city and urban problems. (3)

Urban encounter to effect social change. (1)

Radical communal living; a community of concern. (4)

Uncertain. (1)

In the first weeks more energy and frustration were expended over the issue of purpose than over any other, to very little effect. The situation was characterized more by misunderstanding, lack of communication, and differing opinions than by a shared recognition of that to which the group was committed. It could be objected that any member who was admitted to such a program should be willing to accept a basic definition of intention and goals. At first glance such a suggestion seems unquestionable. But experience raises a further question. Is it possible to ask for a realistic commitment from people who have little understanding of the reality to which they are committing themselves? Only the course of events can reveal those who can endure and those who cannot. For this reason any venture in communal living is bound to have casualties.

As was to be expected, the level of commitment varied enormously. For one or two members the program was seen as primarily providing them with cheap accommodation in Chicago. Others were more interested in the chance to test new freedoms or to experiment with different life-styles. Some came in search of succor for their hurts. Others, more secure, were determined to take on the city, and they expected the Community to act as one body in this estimable project. None of this was apparent in the initial period of the Community's life as, buoyed up with the excitement of a new venture, members took each other at face value, and trustingly proceeded upon their own perception of the adventure, living out of their hopes of what the journey would bring.

Matters of Policy

Before we proceed to an account of the rude awakening that followed, it is necessary to make explicit some of the givens that determined to a considerable extent what happened.

1. First, it was a major decision of policy that the Community be located in one house, rented for the duration of the Community's life. This three-storied edifice, situated in Lincoln Park, a short distance from the Old

Town area, was home for nine members of the Community, although this number rose and fell during the course of the year. Other Community members lived elsewhere but came in for meetings. Included in the latter group were the staff personnel of the Academy. This physical environment exerted a decisive influence on relationships within the Community.

2. A second matter of policy involved the appointment of a staff member of the Academy as tutor, resource person, participating member, and representative of the Academy's interest in the venture. The leadership role exercised by this member was largely influenced by another wise and creative policy decision.

3. The Academy agreed that the Community had the power and the responsibility to "write its own agenda." Almost all that followed in the way of formal educational methodology flowed from this one basic decision.

4. The fourth "given" was the acceptance by the Community that formal meetings should be held twice a week, initially on Mondays and Thursdays, and later on Thursdays and Sundays. These meetings were regarded as mandatory. Any person willfully absent from one of these gatherings was called to account. In this no concessions were made to persons. All members operated under the same rubric. At a minimum level, commitment was defined as being present at all meetings of the Community. It was a tangible test of a person's interest in, and concern for, the life of the group. This requirement was not unambiguously affirmed in practice and was sometimes questioned in theory, but the group set it as a standard from which members choose not to deviate.

At the beginning, all that could be claimed with assurance was that most members would be present at a group meeting two evenings a week.

THE COMMUNITY'S DEVELOPMENT

What follows is an interpretative analysis of the Community's life that is to be viewed in the light of three motifs:

The Need to Survive
The Search for Place
The Awareness of Time

Each motif was present in all phases of the process, but each in turn enjoyed a season of dominance. There was a natural progression from the need to stay alive in a new environment, to a concentration upon the ecology of that environment, to a sharpened sense of time. In the flow of the Community's life these stages were not immediately apparent. Only subsequently was it possible to reflect upon the process and draw from it the elements that present themselves to our scrutiny.

Such a developmental movement is believed to be unavoidable in any Community that shares the same basic characteristics as the Community for Urban Encounter.

The Need to Survive

The first gatherings of the group quickly gave birth to the major issues that the Community was to confront throughout the duration of its life. Over against the genuine desire to learn about the city was a deep and pervasive mistrust of the soulless power that determined the fate of thousands of members of the urban environment. The purely technical aspects of man's social environment, the industrial and technological factors that determine man's social existence, were not so much appreciated for their benefits as feared as a real and present threat to the personal.

Inescapably the mechanistic accomplishments of urban life determined in some measure the view that each person had of himself. Many Community members saw themselves as objects manipulated by the System, adjusted to accept what was an unhappy and intolerable situation, programmed to respond socially without genuine freedom, and totally powerless to bring off any creative change. To them the objective consciousness of American society was most brutally symbolized in the harsh realities of Chicago.

The initial questionnaire raised the query, "What are the basic needs of the city in your opinion?" Included in the responses were: new understanding of organizations and fuller participation by the people in the exercise of power; a sustained effort to tackle the problems of racism, housing, and sanitation; investigation of political offices and law-enforcing bodies. But over the whole appeared one word—humanization.

Observers of the youth scene have pointed to the alienation of the youth culture as springing from a conviction that the developing style of modern technocratic society is against the genuine human interest of the people who are the recipients of its gifts. The young have seen it as their mission to purge science, technology, and civil institutions of a seemingly Olympian indifference to human need. Their deep-seated fear is that as the wheels of scientific rationality roll, human beings are being crushed beneath the machine. The individual appears to be expendable.

The strong current of disenchantment does not represent a rejection of industrial society as such but the values it has spawned. Nor is the anger of the young directed at society as such but at the antiseptic, sterilized remote authority of the System which represents to them all that is negative, inhuman, and unfeeling. An authority, to take but one illustration, which dictates that a young man must go to fight a war he believes to be immoral, against a people who have no military designs against the United States.

The members of the Community for Urban Encounter shared with the general youth culture this same protest against the inhumanity of the System in which they were growing up. But if there was one word that gathered together the prevailing feeling of the group, it was a sense of powerlessness.

Despite what members said, every effort to get them involved in the city's problems failed. As was to be expected, one of the meeting nights was devoted to matters of detail that inevitably arise when a group of strangers set up house together. The other meeting night, however, was to be spent in reflecting upon the involvement of members in the city. It was planned to bring in speakers where necessary, but the basic resource was to be the members' own experience of living and working in the city.

But meeting followed meeting for over two months without this reflective process occurring. Many hours were spent fruitlessly discussing what project the Community could undertake, but unanimity was impossible to obtain. In the light of the results of the questionnaire it is not surprising that with such divergent agendas no common agreement could be reached. Much of this early debate centered around the basic question of whether the group should be more concerned for the life of the city than for the inner reality of the Community's life.

While this discussion raged, people who were designated to lead discussion on their own action in the city failed to come prepared. Others had not "plugged in" yet but were about to do so. Still others had no intention of getting involved anywhere in particular but called for an overview of the city. Others, metaphorically speaking, assumed the fetal position and waited. Like the cars caught in the snowdrifts outside, the Community was spinning its wheels dangerously to little effect.

This continual avoidance of doing exactly what the Community said it existed to do became so obvious that one night a halt was called. *What was happening?* Out of the discussion emerged the understanding that the powerlessness of the group before the System was but a reflection of a powerlessness most members felt about themselves.

They were not the free people that their words suggested. They were a long way from having the inner resources necessary really to engage in the risk and hard work of social change. They were in truth struggling to survive as persons. Inwardly they were in a state of siege, a Civil War feeding out to the world propaganda that at the front all was well, when the true state of affairs was vastly different.

An honest recognition of this situation brought an immediate flood of relief. Not all members were so immobilized by inner anxieties, but the majority were. Once the truth was before the group, it was possible to trace this covert struggle for survival in other areas. The ability to make a firm decision about anything eluded the group for innumerable meetings. But it was an illustration of the deep anxiety that members had about themselves and their ability to cope in a strange environment among strangers.

As the group improved in trust, decisions were made more quickly, but they were carefully recorded and minutes of the meetings distributed. Also, minutes of meetings were needed because few members stuck to the decisions that had been made. Memory was astonishingly short-lived in some cases.

It was a period lived under the law, because the capacity to trust others and to attempt new ways of acting had not developed. Most of the decisions recorded in the minutes reflect the tension between the individual's need for self-protection and the Community's requirements that demanded definite sacrifices, mutual adjustments, and compromise.

The end of the initial struggle was signified by the recognition of the group that minutes of meetings were no longer necessary. After three months the need and practice of taking minutes disappeared. A feeling of belonging together, of being committed to each other, overwhelmed the early sense of having to defend oneself in a potentially hostile environment. An exercise undertaken in this first phase bears this out. Members were asked to complete the sentence, "Living in Community is like . . ." Some of the answers proved illuminating because it was possible to correlate a person's behavior with the image the answers had offered.

Living in Community is like . . . being one leg of a
confused octopus.

. . . not knowing where
you are going.

. . . being in the cage at
a zoo—a friendly
zoo????

. . . living in a prison
without bars.

. . . swimming in a chlorinated pool.

Two observations on these examples are in order. The girl who felt that she was being caged in by the Community decided shortly after that it was not a friendly zoo, and under a combination of internal and external factors, left the Community. The member who spoke of the chlorinated pool explained that he loved swimming but chlorine hurt his eyes, so it was often necessary to get out of the pool. He acted this way in relation to the Community, leaving the house on Friday night and returning late Sunday evening.

To have negotiated this period of the life of the Community successfully was no small accomplishment. But a measure of trust and a growing intimacy bound the members together more strongly because of the turbulence through which they had traveled. The Slough of Despond was behind them. After Christmas, and a week's absence from each other, the group reassembled with high expectancy, dedicated to persisting in the venture and determined to bring off an enterprise of significance.

Thus the second phase began. But the direction had been radically altered. We were no longer committed to an Action-Reflection Model which had guided the group's thinking to this point. The concern was to wrestle with the inability, which members had voiced, to deal with themselves. Resource for the group became the group's own experience, both individual and collective. A deeper concern for the internal life of the Community began to manifest itself as the second phase began.

The Search for Place

In considering the ramifications of the concept of Place, we draw attention to a phenomenon shared by most forms of higher life. Animals seek to establish their "territory" and ceaselessly patrol a particular stamping ground from which they normally will not stray. All societies, whether primitive or sophisticated in development, preserve some places as especially sacred. At the very least they invest with special significance some monuments or places of historic interest that symbolize the deepest aspirations of the culture. Each youth gang jealously guards its own turf.

The relationship of oneself to a particular place, whether treasured in memory (such as one's childhood home or a parent's grave), established in the present, or projected into the future (that dream house), is a crucial element in human existence. It has been suggested that large companies keep their young executives moving every few years so that they have no chance to put down deep roots. Their loyalty as a consequence is directed toward the company rather than toward a particular place.

The concept of Place is more than a geographical one.

It symbolizes the psychological life space that each person must have in order to feel secure in venturing into unfamiliar situations. As Kurt Lewin suggests, all representations of psychological life space are based on the fundamental conception of a particular person in a particular environment. However the details of the boundary between the environment and the person are worked out, the central conception is one of relative "Position." Thus the equation person-environment and "belongingness-to" either the person or the environment define the spatial reality of the individual.

The idea then is to be viewed as a psychobiological reality. While the relationships are dynamic, subject to frequent change, and for the most part remain eternally elusive, the structure of a person's world is determined by the elements of the life space in which he finds himself, just as a river is shaped by the banks between which it flows in its course.

When young people today are described as dislocated in society the designation may be taken with some seriousness. Most young people see themselves as deprived of a meaningful world in which they can with integrity locate themselves. If their alienation springs from a conviction that "authority," however conceived, is antithetical to their search for the Personal, their dislocation stems from a recognition that there is no place to go where one might be free to experiment with the deepest communality of human experience. Freud's comment that being a Jew gave him a clear consciousness of inner identity illumines how important this internal sense of belonging is, even if it defies precise description. Perhaps the best contemporary illustration of this hunger for a sympathetic community is the hippie communes.

The widespread interest in communal living and tribal existence within the youth culture may have its origins in this very lack of congenial life space. The heroes of *Easy Rider,* like their TV counterpart Bronson, have no place to lay their heads. As the words of a song popular among the young put it, "There's a place for us . . . somewhere a place for us . . . somewhere, someday . . . somewhere." Oddly enough, a favorite novel among the members of the Community bore the title *Stranger in a Strange Land.*

Protests over the pollution of the natural environment illustrate a growing contemporary awareness that man cannot exist in an environment that has been robbed of its naturalness and stripped of its beauty. The "new morality" may be an internal illustration of the same drive to find a centeredness, created in relationships that will invest each individual's life with meaning. Love is a space-binding as well as a space-creating emotion. It establishes the internal reality of "home."

This brief discussion of life space is a necessary precondition for penetrating with understanding into the inner significance of the second phase of the Community's life. The psychological depths of having a place are related to the awareness of the meaning of the Personal. In one sense the boundaries of what is "mine" define the limits of the person. Living in a communal environment helps the person to extend the boundaries to include others, so that the opportunity provided by a community of trust is an extended ego and, as a consequence, a growing realization of personal identity and what *I mean* in relationships. That involves growth, a process of change in a new becoming.

In the case of the Community, openness was possible only when the early feeling of threat was removed and members felt able to reveal their true selves to each other without fear of hurt or betrayal.

One negative and one positive illustration will serve to demonstrate the point. One of the girls living in the house, who found it difficult to share with the group its newfound interest in the inner life of the Community, began to withdraw in the meetings. Although she was almost always present, her participation was minimal. At the same time that her participation became less, she began to decorate her room in her favorite color. The rug, the bedspread, the curtains, the lampshade, the decorations were all the same color. To survive in the house in a situation that became increasingly threatening, this member responded by creating in her own immediate intimate environment a locale of such distinctiveness that she was constantly reinforced in her sense of self-worth when she left the others and entered her room. The second illustration concerns one of the boys who was more disoriented in his personal life and behavior than most of the other members. On one occasion he obtained a large supply of ticker tape which he piled on the basement floor and used as a bed. The Community referred to it affectionately as "the nest." Only after some attention had been paid to this member's needs was the ticker tape one fateful day swept aside from the center of the basement and a bed procured that, for the most part, served as an alternative. But the correlation between this member's growing sense of belonging and the removal of this symbol of impermanence was striking.

The house had begun to take on the atmosphere of a

nourishing and sustaining environment that offered possibilities of freedom and security, essential preconditions for change and growth. In this phase the Community's life became noticeably more intense, charged with a spirit of inquiry and renewed with a sense of hope. Several collages appeared on the walls, expressive of this new sense of belonging, and verbal symbols began to emerge around which the group rallied.

The first phase of the Community had furnished the group with the word "Fork" which functioned as a negative symbol and as a thinly disguised euphemism used in moments of frustration.

The second phase gave birth to "Berfunkling." Whatever that meant, and no one could say precisely what it did mean, it was a profound and positive symbol of the most real and significant moments of the Community's life. When we were really down to it, dealing with problems or issues without pretense or sham, we were "berfunkling."

It was during this period that the first clear signs of the impact of living in Community began to emerge. The honesty and directness of encounter forced many Community members to face reality in a way they had not done before. Determined efforts were made to deal with the problems that unavoidably arose in the group's relationships, and many individuals found that their glib rhetoric could not stand before the searching inquiry of other members who demanded a consistency in the relationship of actions and words.

Members learned with astonishment how many of their number had sought professional help, how inadequate their attempts to handle tensions were, how far from being the liberated and concerned persons they imagined themselves to be. The ability to be open to the group developed slowly. With self-disclosure came a measure of release from anxiety.

Communication became a crucial concern, not because it was deemed a desirable feature but because it was germane to the health of the Community. As people began to test the acceptance of the group, they began to grow in personal acceptance. Progress was not easy, because the capacity to trust was difficult to find when much of one's experience has taught that no one can be trusted. It was a perilous enterprise that produced several disasters as well as many small triumphs.

In one case the risk was too great. One of the boys confessed to the group that he could not be open to the Community. Despite every effort to resolve the difficulty, he finally withdrew from the project. But in going he carried with him the clear awareness that he needed professional help to deal with relationships at more than an instrumental level. The growing recognition of their need for each other, however, became stronger in the other members. During this period a banner appeared on the wall with the plea, "Push or pull or get out of the way."

The trumpet made no uncertain sound. One had to become deeply involved. This was a place where one had to invest time and effort. The house had become a habitat which, through struggle and sometimes pain, offered possibilities of growth and wholeness, a stern yet embracing environment of concern, love, and hope that made available new ways of being human, new patterns of response, space to become truly oneself. Perhaps one of the girls said more than she knew when she wrote: "Some decisions are relatively unimportant. Where you are is not."

The Awareness of Time

The third phase of the Community's life was dominated by the motif of Time. From one point of view it was simply the brute fact of the end of the program. Long before the end, discussions arose about reentry problems, the most appropriate way the Community might finish, and what lay before them as they moved on.

Paradoxically, this common sense of the shortness of time resulted in an increased urgency on the one hand and a movement of withdrawal back into safe confines on the other. This latter movement sprang from the self-protective instinct that suggests to us all that as time is short, there is no use getting more deeply involved. In this way we are seduced into retreat by the thief of time. Our chance to invest what time we do have with richer meaning is lost. The recognition of the self-defeating nature of withdrawal increased the general determination to make every last moment count for something. But the ambivalence remained.

However, this serial understanding of time was secondary to a qualitative dimension within time. The concern here was for meaning and purpose. As with Benjamin in *The Graduate,* the most urgent question before the members of the group was the question, "What are you going to do?"

The inability to find some significant meaning in the life process results in a lack of direction and, correspondingly, in a loss of the sense of personal destiny. A feeling of hopelessness, that nothing is really important, immobilizes the creative powers of the individual. If there is no open future for us, it is unlikely that any kind of purpose will manifest itself in the ebb and flow of the person's life. Life becomes reduced to random events obedient to the flux of circumstances. In such a predicament a person may easily lose the sense of who he is.

Out of this awareness the group came to view time as a double reality, both as the "Now" thing, which all seem to predicate concerning the world view of the current generation, and also as that other theme of a viable future.

Margaret Mead, among others, has argued that for the young the future is now. Behind this judgment lies the conviction that today's young people live out of a new mode of experiencing and viewing the world that followed the atomic bomb blasts at the end of the Second World War. The world is known to be destructible, and human life as well. In addition, the multidimensional mass media have made communication an instantaneous event. The young have responded by living with Dionysian exuberance in the present. Realistically they cannot expect that the world will always continue. They seek therefore to drain the cup of experience, living as fully as they can in the present, for there might not be a tomorrow. Negatively, this time sense can be seen as a reaction to the Protestant ethic so dominant in American society, which urges the postponement of present pleasures for the sake of a rich and honorable future when the fruits of a hardworking and righteous life can be enjoyed. Positively, it is a celebration of the dance of life itself, a festivity to joy, a shout of sheer delight for being alive.

Apparently, however, the edge of desperateness present in this deification of the Now has escaped the adults, who, viewing the youth scene from the security of years, applaud youth's vitality and their wish for freedom and abandon. The life of the Community, which has been offered as a microcosm of the youth culture itself, does not support this one-dimensional view captured in the phrase, "The future is now."

If the revolt against an established system of meaning is to be a creative one, it needs to occur in the name of some other scheme that offers an interpretation of the whole and provides, in the process, a horizon of "ultimate" significance. This is not to deny the obvious commitment to the present. For the young people in the Community, as well as for their peers beyond, present anxieties take precedence over possible future needs. Process is far more crucial than content. Participation is prized above disengagement. The spontaneous is delightfully prior to the planned. What the group creates takes prominence over any nature of things that might, or might not, happen to exist.

But despite this the young cannot forget that they have themselves on their hands. The future must be considered because it will not go away. Even the prolonged moratorium of adolescence must end someday. And because they know this they worry about the future.

A discussion on one occasion as to why young people use drugs elicited from the Community the intriguing consensus that the dope addict has rejected the future. The reasons suggested included the idea that not only does he lack centeredness as a person but he is unable to accept an ambiguous reality. As one of the group, who exists on the fringe of the drug subculture, put it, "To come to grips with your ego you have to accept your ultimate finiteness."

Inescapably the question of meaning poses itself. The existential urgency of this need for a purposeful direction was communicated to the group by one member, as she struggled to share her dilemma, in this way: "Right now I feel completely disconnected. I don't know where I'm going. Going back home . . . going no place. . . . It seems the same thing."

The group recognized that the question that was thrown up again and again was the question of vocation. "What can I do?" "What might I become?" The trickle became a flood after one member confessed to the group that he realized he was wasting his time and talents. He asked their help to find a job worth doing.

Two of the members who had dropped out of college began taking steps to go back to school. Another member seized firmly the idea of a vocational security in education. Other members began to take seriously questions that they had turned aside from many years before. All of this, it is claimed, pointed to a rediscovered awareness of time and its significance.

But the most startling illustration of the liberation effected by the Community was the growing consensus that it was time to move on, time to begin acting, time to ask, "What are we going to do about the city?" Seemingly the wheel had come full circle. Someone passed the observation that "Community tells a man who he is." If the word "Community" can be read as referring to the small group whose life has concerned us here, then unquestionably the experience of life in the Community had fulfilled this function for most members.

The clarification of identity freed some members to make new commitments. The need for a sense of coherence, personal integration, and wholeness had been met in the warm, accepting environment of the Community. Part of this inner strength came from an ability to tolerate ambiguity in men's social existence and to accept ambivalence in oneself. What bound these together was a principle that enabled members to transcend the many threats to their person that before the journey would have totally disarmed them.

The presupposition of the whole venture was the symbolic significance of the word "Community." It has been used in a purely instrumental sense in the present discussion, but it was far more than this for the group. It came to represent for each member his own warrant as a person. To make it in this kind of situation is in principle to make it in any situation that life can present. They had, because of "Community," begun the movement from the penultimate statement, "I am" to the final affirmation of the mature person, "I am able."

It was this realization which brought a new sense of freedom. When members began to express a concern for the city, they were not repudiating the months of living together, focused on themselves, but testifying to its creative effect. The force of these remarks can best be illustrated by the words of Community members themselves. The following comments arose in a general discussion in the final phase of the Community's existence:

BRUCE: "I want to see a gradual change in the present program. I don't know what exactly. I want to get into new groups, theater groups, political groups. We have become too dependent upon the house. We need to widen our score."

ANDY: "But we have had a unique experience which most people haven't had."

JACK: "I sense a hell of a long way in people's ability to listen to each other."

BRUCE: "Yes, but we need to get people moving out now. Take Karen." (Karen was absent from the meeting.)

DIANE: "For Karen this has been as valuable a year as one of my years in college."

JACK: "No Community can ignore personal needs. What would we do with people like Karen who are not able to handle an issue-oriented group?"

LISA: "They must know they want that."

KEVIN: "We are starting to wake up corporately."

TERRY: "People have a commitment here which is constantly called into question. You've got to be able to live with it. This motivates you to take action in relation to other commitments."

JACK: "That's great! It's a process of holding us up against ourselves."

KEVIN: "The Community is a dipstick for life. I've had an identity crisis every day since I moved in here. Some I managed to get the better of, some not. I have to examine myself again and again."

LISA: "It's a calling into question whether you are doing something with yourself for your own sake."

JACK: "For me it's been a maintenance thing. It's enabled me to make it through a very difficult time."

LISA: "I'm not sure what it's doing, but now I have more a future vision than a past. I have not always been able to ask the straight honest question, but now there is a feeling of immediacy. You have to do it now. It's acting out yourself. It's manifesting yourself on a personal and relational level."

TERRY: "It's a great growing-up experience."

LISA: "I guess the atmosphere gives you the freedom to demand explanation."

TERRY: "When I come home at night I cannot sit down and watch TV and be content like I did last year."

DIANE: "That's nothing! For seven years I would come home from work . . . sleep . . . eat . . . read a book . . . and then go back to sleep."

KEVIN: "The Community really shocked us out of our aimlessness."

TERRY: "I have a feeling of self-worth I didn't have before."

BRUCE: "Yeah, I just sat around and watched the tube. I notice a difference in my attitude to people in particular."

LISA: "Well, if we're talking about a sense of purpose, which we seem to have discovered, I'm going back to school. It's just a question of whether it will be part time or full time."

JACK: (*Facetiously*) "So now you are going back to life!"

(*General laughter.*)

CONCLUSIONS

This analysis of the life of the Community for Urban Encounter has been woven around the motifs of Survival, Place, and Time, which seemed to interpret the movement of the group's existence. These motifs continued throughout to reassert themselves. Some members failed to move with the majority of the group, so that they continued to wrestle with "Survival" or "Place" after the others had turned their attention to other concerns and different questions. The reality was a mobile and continually ambiguous situation that was far from being as clear-cut as the analysis might suggest.

But what is being argued is that, given a similar model for Community living, the same three phases will inevitably emerge.*

---

* In quest for further understanding of this situation an examination of institutions using an Action-Reflection Model was undertaken. It soon became apparent that such enterprises could continue to maintain their efficiency only as long as the members of the Community or Order were given tasks beyond their capacity to complete. By keeping people externally busy, no time was available to consider the personal problems of those involved, and for many participants this very rigidity of structure was affirmed precisely because it gave little chance to participants to worry about their personal tensions. Once the pressure was relieved, however, the repressed personal anxieties erupted to the surface like a reactivated Vesuvius.

Until each motif, in its moment of ascendancy, has been dealt with, a Community cannot move on to new tasks. Different Communities may pass through the stages more rapidly and be free to focus on task-oriented activities much earlier, but that is only a matter of relative speed of progression.

It might be argued in opposition to this point of view that the Community described is an atypical one and that what is claimed has no validity beyond this particular group. No one can deny the force of this objection, and much more data from different Communities would need to be gathered to support the thesis. However, some reply is possible.

1. The Community represented as diverse a selection of young people as could be expected. They did not represent either a body of thoughtful young people already coalesced around several clearly defined centers or a group that totally lacked any sense of responsibility. It has already been indicated that they were not united in a common sense of purpose. Initially, members pursued goals, many of which were antithetical to each other.

2. A second response would suggest that, as far as possible, the motifs discussed were illustrated from the general youth culture itself. The ideas of Survival, Place, and Time, as used here, have their negative counterparts in words used continually to describe the mood of the young—alienation, dislocation, aimlessness.

The strength of this organizing typology is that its key concepts are primal ones that apply to human existence as such. *Thus it may be possible, theoretically speaking, to use these central motifs to help interpret the life of any group that shares some of the major characteristics of the Community for Urban Encounter. To that degree this Community experiment may function as a paradigm against which all such communal ventures may choose to test themselves.*

Several questions remain. Are there only three phases? Why not a fourth, or more? Or to put the same question in another way, What follows the third phase? The question calls forth two observations.

1. If another mode of communal togetherness could be symbolized, it would be in the idea of Celebration. In the last weeks, as the journey came to an end, a sense of accomplishment and joy pervaded the Community's life. The creative finale of the Community, with its grief and gladness, had about it an ecstatic element that transcended the particular emotions of the time and transmuted the whole process into an occasion of reverence and gratitude.

2. Any fourth phase, if the term can be properly used, lies beyond the Community qua Community. If the members of the group are now truly free, then this freedom will express itself in new commitments, a renewed sense of purpose, a zest for living and serving which is the outflow of their own joy and response to that which they were given in the year of their life together. That is the hope the organizers of the project cherish.

THE SEARCH FOR VISION

One final dimension remains. At the beginning the claim was made that there was a tacit unity in this disparate group of individuals, which was described as a seeking after some unifying vision. It was argued that when a man is free from the struggle to survive, he is able to build some realistic life-style consistent with the demands of life. In the symbol of Place there is a necessary moment of rest without which no person can exist. The symbol of Time, by contrast, is expressive of the other moment of continual change. Thus the human experiences of being and becoming are woven together.

The creative unity of these two modes of existence is reinforced when "creative memory" binds them together. Out of this unity a viable future is born. It is that gestalt of experience which offers a way of understanding the word "Vision." Out of the treasured memory of a particular past, sustained by a deep personal sense of self-worth, the individual trusts that for him (and, in principal, for all men) there is an imaginable future which calls forth his most dedicated energies and lures him on to a destiny, which, in spite of and in the midst of ambiguity, defines for him who he really is. As Rilke suggests, in memory one looks back on an irrevocable year of anguish and vision and prayer. We hope, at journey's end, to have come home to a realization of our true selves.

II

DIARY
OF THE COMMUNITY'S LIFE

DIANE: Diane had traveled from New York to join the Community. She spent her year teaching in a ghetto school on the South side of Chicago. Always cheerful and hardworking, Diane, the oldest member of the group, was one of the members who gave the Community stability. Committed to the church, she received considerable teasing from the others about her affiliation. The Community called into question many of the stereotypes that Diane had cherished. She became more realistic in her view of life.

LISA: Lisa was tall, blond, and sympathetic by nature. The need to establish independence from home was Lisa's strongest drive, and she struggled in the Community to become her own person. Lisa was searching for a vocation, having dropped out of school for the duration of the Community's life. She was vulnerable to hurt and in need of the support of the Community. During the year, Lisa was employed as a secretary in a small publishing firm.

CINDY: Bright, vivacious, talkative when not in group meetings, Cindy was employed as a social worker for the Cook County Department of Public Welfare. Constantly busy and active elsewhere, Cindy gave little to the Community meetings. She seemed unable to balance a concern for social transformation with a productive personal existence in the Community and unable to accept the fact that others did not share her passion for social involvement. Her social activism added a dimension to the life of the Community that well might have been lacking without her.

KAREN: Karen was highly intelligent, articulate, and personally disoriented. She sought from the Community an acceptance and healing which welled out of the deeply personal. Past hurts made her oversensitive to misunderstanding. Karen sought some personal integrity of being and found it difficult to tolerate failure or ambiguity easily. Her contribution to the Community was a clear-sighted awareness of the threat that present society posed to the development of a fully human existence.

JANE:

Jane was withdrawn, frightened by groups of people, and unable to feel secure in many situations encountered in the house. Jane had several jobs, was unable to define what she wanted from the Community. After an initial attempt to enter into the life of the group, she left after three months.

DAWN:

A graduate student studying for her master's degree in medical school, Dawn was attractive, warm, and concerned about social issues. Because of increased work pressures, as well as a promotion to laboratory assistant, Dawn was forced to leave the Community after three months. Her interest, however, was more in a socially active Community. In her going the Community lost a strong voice for a concerned engagement with the problems of the city.

GARY:

Very personable, intellectual, and aggressive, Gary was the product of an unhappy home situation. Simultaneously wanting and not wanting the Community, accepting and aggressive, Gary exerted a negative influence on the Community's life. Hostility about his past spilled over in the form of rage at others and at himself. After a conflict with Karen, Gary left the Community. A final-year student at a downtown university, Gary was unable to tolerate opposition, despite his recognition that he needed others. His relationship with the Community remained cordial.

ANDY: Andy was employed in a Community organization on the Northwest side of Chicago. Bearded, shy, and yet occasionally eruptive in manner, Andy was appreciative and concerned for the welfare of human beings. Andy's need was a group with which he could celebrate, and as he continued in the Community a difficulty in speaking clearly disappeared as he gained more confidence. Seven months after the Community began, Andy was married and ceased to be a participating member.

TERRY: Bearded, long-haired, 6'5", Terry was a conscientious objector doing alternative service in a hospital. The most gentle of the Community members, Terry, like Diane, was a faithful and reliable participant whose contribution and concern for others was unquestioned. Struggling to express himself more fully and to find independence from his parents, Terry learned to become more aggressive and self-assured during the year.

KEVIN: Like Andy and Lisa, Kevin was the child of a clergyman. Working in the same hospital as Terry, and seeking conscientious objector status, Kevin had no clear idea of what to do with his life. He was addicted to an electric guitar, a symbol of some significance to him, and was involved in the use of mild drugs. Bearded, intelligent, creative, and unreliable, Kevin was an example of the searching dropout. The youngest member of the Community (eighteen), Kevin began to feel during the course of the year that he could really become a musician.

BRUCE: A college dropout, Bruce was working in a hospital raising money to complete his degree. In the meantime he was, to use his own words, "sorting himself out." Also fighting an unhappy past, Bruce was perceptive, apt to be dogmatic, concerned for the Community, and dependent upon its warmth and security. Bruce was fiercely against drugs, which meant that he, Kevin, and Graham often came into conflict over that issue. For Bruce every issue was brought down to the concrete, and he argued with intense feeling.

GRAHAM: Graham came to the Community not as a member initially but with Terry and

Kevin with whom he had roomed to that time. Good-looking and charming, Graham was the most dislocated member of the Community who, in the early stages, sought solace in drugs or alcohol or women. Possessing many gifts, Graham was unable to function efficiently because of the constant pressure of a family situation of the worst kind. He found a measure of escape in hedonistic pursuits. Employed by a computer firm as a supervisor, Graham earned more than other Community members, but he worked night shift and was often unable to attend meetings.

JIM:

Jim Reid (Jack in the Diary entries), initiator of the project, forty years of age, father of five children, was the representative of the Northside Lay Academy. Accepting, able to live with ambiguity, Jim participated as any other member. Having a commitment to social action, Jim found it difficult to accept the fact that the Community could not function with the proposed Action-Reflection Model of social engagement. He wrestled with this problem existentially, sometimes affirming, always seeking to understand.

DENHAM:

An Australian engaged in doctoral studies in Chicago, Denham was tutor to the group and recorder of the group's life. Denham was very much involved in the life of the Community and constantly held before the group the need to test what was said with the behavior of the speaker. "Say what you want, but we shall watch what you do." Counselor and enabler to the group, Denham was married and, like Jim, lived outside the Community house.

The following Diary entries were written after each Community meeting and record events as well as reflections upon what occurred. Much else happened that was not included, for in each case the dominant impression was sought as a means of entering into the most significant moments of the Community experience. In some cases several incidents that took place at the one meeting are included. The events develop chronologically.

In order to preserve anonymity, the names of Community members have been changed and some measure of obscurity has been retained in the Diary entries. But what is printed is the journal that Community members themselves explored at the end of each month.

Since our first meeting a week ago, several gatherings have taken place. The policy decision to allow the Community to order its own life has been decisive for the early development of the Community. It has meant the putting aside of formal curricula, and the group "writes its own agenda." The test will be whether this decision can be used creatively. Clearly, however, the members of the Community affirm this principle. They have a right to order their own life.

Not surprisingly, early tensions were created because of the Individual-Community polarity that Tillich says is a basic polarity in Existence. Should the individual be free "to do his own thing"? Should not the Community act as a united body? It is apparent that at times the individual must resist the will of the Community (although I hope better explanations for doing so are advanced in the future than the vague, "I have my reasons"), and times when, for the sake of the Community, the individual must make some personal sacrifice. This is always a matter of balance, and it is to be hoped that we are mature enough to make concessions where they are most needed. The destructive side of this tension, however, has revealed itself when an individual holds the group to blackmail—"Without me you cannot move, and I will not agree." Or the other side of the same coin— the group ignoring an individual who feels deeply about an issue and does not agree with the Community mind on it. We must be honest here, and understanding. At this stage I ask the question, Can we be open? I hope we can.

The house must surely be a plus. Those who live in the family have a valuable chance to learn the art of compromise and what trust and acceptance really are. Nothing wishy-washy there, and the members are handling their internal problems splendidly so far. But there are other reasons. There is a place to go that is always available. No problems arise about obtaining a mutual meeting place. We can eat and share together. The house is becoming "our place," and I don't think those who live in it resent that other Community members feel that way about it. Nor is there any gap between house members and the Community. Despite its strains and stresses, I believe that locating the Community in a house has been a significant decision that will finally prove most creative.

Tonight a decision was taken. Three cheers for that! For several weeks we have been unable to get a consensus on anything. We meet on two evenings a week—Monday and Thursday. Behind that decision, however, lies a serious division of purpose. In defining the present need of the group, some press for "Sensitivity Training," others for "Action-Reflection." The compromise reached is that on Mondays the Community gathers for "Nurture," to use a traditional term. Thursdays the focus is upon its "Mission" and involvement in the urban scene. Here is a predictable case where the need for compromise appears. It could have been on a hundred and one other matters, but tensions arose on this particular difference of opinion and both sides have a point. The fact that *all* accepted a compromise revealed a spirit of cooperation, a recognition of the need for compromise, and a growing maturity. It was not surprising, therefore, that we reached agreement at last on the style of the proposed retreat weekend that has been under discussion. As for the weekend, I see it as necessary just now and believe it will contribute much to our enlarging understanding of what we are in together.

A problem tonight. After we had spent long hours resolving the conflict about what we should do, the result of three weeks of haggling, at the next meeting Rachel, who had not been at the previous meeting, took us back through the same discussion again. Her questions were to the point, but many of the group who had been frustrated last week, and then given some hope, were even more frustrated by the repeat discussion on the same matter. There is a matter of policy here, I think, which this incident reveals. Should people be totally "in" or totally "out"? When some members, like Rachel, are coming only to occasional meetings, they disrupt the flow of the Community's life. This means that the Community is constantly going back on its tracks in order to bring absent members up to date, with a consequent increased threshold of frustration. Perhaps on this matter the weekend will provide a chance for people to examine their commitment. Barry, for example, has weighed the option and is "out."

A similar question about those who are "in" and those who are "out" arose in discussion this evening. Jane has decided not to be a member of the Community but continues to live in the house. Graham, of course, has always had an ambiguous relationship to the Community. What the issue is exactly is hard to determine, but it has definite relatedness to the Community's growth. I did not interpret the discussion as a negative one. But some clarification of people's commitment to the Community needs to occur. I do not think there is any consensus on this matter. Certainly no one wishes to prevent visitors from sitting in and contributing to the discussions. Lisa's contribution, as one example, has been helpful on several occasions. Perhaps the tension centers on the ambiguous relationship of those who are neither clearly in one category nor the other. Visitors are not confusing in their relationships and are naturally welcome. Is this desire for neatness somewhat inhuman or is it a justifiable request of people to declare themselves? Each case, I guess, has to be taken on its own merits.

After six weeks in the house, signs of change have begun. The "Listen, Christian" posters are up. We now have drapes and a green carpet. My own feeling about this environmental change is that it reflects a deepening sense of belonging. The art display was even better! We belong! We share!

We had decided to discuss *Easy Rider* on Thursday night and had done so. Terry, however, argued that the discussion went too long and was a waste of time. His honesty led to a disclosure that confirmed the strong suspicion I had formed. Since the decision to use Thursday night as the evening to focus on the task of the Community, Thursdays have been a total wipe out. The puzzling factor is that people agree to take action during the meetings, but make no effort to do so in practice outside the meetings.

There was a "classic" demonstration tonight of the tension between Community participation and individual noninvolvement. For the last two weeks Cindy has been slowly but unmistakably making it clear that she is uninvolved in the meetings, for reasons that, despite her explanations, are still obscure. The group with some anxiety, concern, and irritation asked her to explain why this was so in order that it might be understood and creatively handled. The response was silence and, it is fair to say, a stubborn setting of the jaw. As Cindy admitted in a rare comment while the group thrashed around the problem, she was protecting herself. No sharing occurred. The group remained frustrated. Cindy maintained silence. The meeting finally ended in some disarray, and it was no surprise to hear that on the weekend some of the Community stayed up all night in heated but therapeutic conversation. Cindy remains intransigent.

A curious issue that we return to again and again, even after two months, is the matter of people living in the house who make no contribution to the Community, nor are committed to its life. I am of the opinion that such a situation should be avoided in the future if possible. Too much time is lost reworking old ground. Before a person enters the house, the terms of the "contract" should be made clear. Involvement means . . . In that way some guidelines can be set within which freedom may be gained. Without any guidelines anarchy results, although the Community is working manfully at dealing with the situation.

"Thursday night I had an encounter session with Graham, one of the greatest things that happened to me. I really came out! He must have something on the ball from this Community to do that! Since then I am a changed person. Even my roommate noticed the difference . . . and until now she had been antagonistic to the Community."

In this fashion did Lisa reveal to us that reconciliation and hope are working in us. A cause for celebration—and of no small proportions at that! The last six weeks have been rough on us all.

Understandably the group frustration rises when, after a decision has been made, the matter is brought up again for consideration. Such a process appears inevitable, however, until all members consent together to the spirit as well as to the letter of the "law."

"Do we trust people's reasons for being absent from meetings or not? That is the question. My feeling tonight is that I've been irresponsible in not calling Kevin when he left for a date on a meeting night. I guess part of my responsibility is to make other people responsible." Gary voiced succinctly a major principle of collective responsibility that the group has come to affirm.

Tonight Jane expressed a not uncommon ambivalence —she had her own concerns that have made her a non-participant in the group and yet she needs the Community badly. I believe some measure of understanding and acceptance emerged over the weekend retreat that made clear also how desperately important the Community is to many members in it. So important is the Community that disharmony is hard to live with and causes considerable pain. On the other hand, other Community members imply that they can "take it or leave it," if they so choose. I wonder if that is the truth. In any case each member is there to serve the Community as much as to be served by the Community. One sows pretty much what one reaps in this situation as in many others. The result of an aloof attitude toward others is likely to result in greater alienation and further isolation. The art of forgiving and the act of forgetting past failure is a precondition of health in the Community.

———

The trip to Washington for the November Moratorium demonstration and the retreat weekend away cemented the group considerably, even if it was through the pain of misunderstanding. Karen made an invaluable offering to the Community at the weekend by being honest and revealing her hurt. She was outraged by the behavior of the boys in Washington. She believed them completely insensitive to her feelings, Gary in particular. Out of that courageous self-disclosure grew a deeper trust. The collage that was created subsequently by Karen as a thankful reaction now adorns the wall in the lounge room, reminding us all that we are beggars to each other, seeking food for our life together. Its central word is HOPE.

———

Since the retreat weekend, there has been a willingness to utilize theater games as a nonverbal expression of communicating meaning. Thus the symbolic dimension is emerging as significant. The uninitiated would make no sense of a shouted, "FORK." But it means many unexpressible things to the Community.

December already, and we seem to be freer to take up external concerns and less subjective interests. Peggy Way is to come and talk with us on social involvement. Operation Breadbasket will enjoy a visit from some Community members next Saturday. A section of Bonhoeffer's *Ethics* was discussed with profit. Is it premature to hope that internal freedom will permit external (to the Community) responsibility?

I felt tonight that I had made the mistake of dominating the discussion, a departure from the role of facilitation that has been acceptable to the group to this stage and seems to be the most responsible way of being present from my point of view. The result was a choking off of the free flow of discussion, and it reminded me again that the goals, expectations, and intentions of the leader are not the most important things to the group. In our Community, at least, the needs of the Community must write the agenda.

In retrospect the most important single point of clarification in the last month has been the recognition that some people will be involved in the city more than others. But it is to be a matter of policy that those who are involved share their experiences and reflections with the whole Community. The trip to Washington served to demonstrate that all could benefit by reflecting on the experiences of a few, thanks to Dawn's persistence in asking questions. In this fashion, opportunity is provided for members of the Community to pursue their varied interests and yet add to the growth and maturity of the whole Community.

With the exception of Graham, most are going home for Christmas, so we meet again in January.

JANUARY

The first gatherings of the Community after the Christmas break demonstrated how much the sense of belonging together had grown since the first meetings three months or so before. Everyone seemed glad to be back, and the absence of several members at the first meeting was experienced as the loss of something fundamentally important, crucial for the proper functioning of the Community.

Graham had a bad trip on acid over Christmas and was found wandering incoherent in the streets. He spent three days in a mental hospital recovering. It is interesting to speculate what Christmas means to people when they have no one to share the season with them. If Graham was alone in the house when Christmas burst upon the world again, then it is understandable that some substitute reality was sought as a way of living with loneliness. The message is, we need people, all of us.

During this evening's discussion, Kevin raised with the group a dilemma that he has been living with for some time. He is considering going to the East Coast "to play guitar" and to stay with a friend who grooves with Kevin's ambitions and interests. But to leave the Community and other established relationships imposed such a strain that he had been unable to decide, so he sought guidance from the group. What followed was a somewhat intensive investigation of Kevin's motives, a questioning of the reality of his self-image, and a view of his capacities. It was painful. It was demanding. It finally crystallized into a decision. Kevin was to stay and take guitar lessons in order to attain the basic skills necessary to match his competence with his dreams.

Two things stood out clearly from this experience. The first was Kevin's courage in risking himself with the group, a decision that resulted in considerable pain and some clarification. The second was the desire of the Community not to tell Kevin what he *wanted* to hear but what he most *needed* to hear. Out of this coalescing of responsible actions, some reality therapy occurred. Is this a paradigm of how the Community should act? Being faithful to itself in demanding a full explanation of a member's motives, and ministering to the needs of that member in the process.

Bruce stamped out of the meeting in anger before all this took place, ostensibly because of the irresponsible behavior of the Community in wasting time. He was right about that, but that was only half the story. It was an occasion for rejoicing that after venting his outraged feelings on Gary outside the group he returned and enabled the group to understand a little of the oppressive load he was carrying. While he was gone, it was like having an arm wrenched out of its socket. Say what we will, it is clear that we have come to care for each other. It is also true that we are far from being sensitive enough to know when people are hurting and so help them express that hurt before it becomes more painful.

Graham, who works night shift, is unable to be present at the meetings. He has also been acting in a way that raises acute problems for other members of the house, particularly over the drug situation. He has agreed under pressure to stop pushing drugs, but that is only a beginning. After we discussed the matter, we decided to switch from Monday-night meetings to Sunday evenings, so that Graham could be present. Although the change places some burden on other members, it seems to be the most creative decision, given all the circumstances.

It is not the big things but the little things that cause the greatest irritation for those living in the house. Ashtrays not emptied, garbage left in the kitchen, the delay in getting the new shower promised by the landlords months ago, the failure of members to pay their money for the retreat weekend now several months past, the borrowing of other people's clothes without permission, the agreement to phone someone and then forgetting to do so—these are the rocks upon which the ship may founder, not the raging storms of intense feelings that always seem to blow themselves out before destruction occurs.

Jane has quietly left us and is living in an apartment nearby with Gavin.

A snatch of conversation—
"The Community is a place to make sense of what is important to you and to try to interact with people . . . It's happened a couple of times without my realizing . . . I think about it after, and realize it . . . I would like to see ourselves as resource. For me, not much is valid outside of what I experience . . . I feel like I'm missing two thirds of what is going on!"

Gary was close to his innermost fears when he confessed to the group, "I'm afraid to risk myself." The greatest gift of the Community to itself will be the creating of that climate of trust in which a member feels free to risk himself.

More wise words—"What is important? I would say finding out what each of us is about. Ideas don't do any good unless you share them. I need to test them against other people to see if they are real."

We need responsibility, not authority.

I had felt for some time that the group has been passive, drifting along with no one taking the initiative for what occurred, so the matter was raised with the group. The consensus was that such was the melancholy truth. Why should that be so? The clearest explanation seemed to be an inability to trust the group's response if someone took the initiative. So it comes back to basic trust again and the fear of betrayal. Erikson was surely right when he suggested that the ability to trust is the cornerstone of personhood.

Diane, who has had no experience of teaching black kids from the ghetto, is finding the going tough. She cannot control the class. Sometimes she had been reduced to tears. It appears that little help is available. I am not sure that the discussions of the situation provided much assistance, but at least Diane knows that the Community cares. It was finally resolved to seek some training for Diane, if such was available, in how to teach in the situation in which she finds herself.

Barry decended upon the Community with a plea for help in the forthcoming strike at Wesley Hospital. We have since learned that he is under threat of losing his job for his unionizing activities. Although the decision was made in December not to become a social-action community, it is apparent that social issues such as this one concern the Community, especially when raised by someone like Barry, who is an adjunct member of the Community, if such a term can be used. Cindy has the concerns of social welfare; Diane, her teaching in a ghetto school; Kevin and Terry, their engagement in the coffeehouse. We are not totally divorced from the world, even though we have debated that question many times.

What is "berfunkling"? Only the Community knows. However inexpressible it is, its meaning is that quality of life and purpose which is concerned for the "deepest down things," in Hopkins' phrase. Another symbol along with "Fork," but this time one filled with potentiality and creative possibilities.

As I reflect on the month of January, the following lines from a childhood poem spring to mind, probably incorrectly recalled. Is it really like this?

There was an old sailor my grandfather knew
Who had so many things which he wanted to do
That, whenever he thought it was time to begin,
He couldn't—because of the state he was in.

That seems to be where we are. Which leads to the sober reflection that all we have is experience itself, the process of living together, the Now of vital communion. There is no end at which we shall presently arrive, no metaphysical guillotine that will descend to trim off our rough human corners and make the package of our strivings neat and ordered. If we cannot grasp what we have now, fragmented, broken, incomplete as it is, then we will grasp nothing at all.

FEBRUARY

The events this month have been shaped and colored by a crisis in relationship that resulted in Karen's packing a suitcase and moving out of the house. It is difficult to pinpoint precisely what caused the argument, but the particular incident appears to be the occasion for, rather than the cause of, the relocation. It was the straw that broke the camel's back. Karen has felt for some time that her willingness to take on many of the household chores, in order to make the Community work, had been taken advantage of by many of the Community members and by Gary in particular. His angry demand for an explanation as to why his supper wasn't ready set off a complicated series of events, the end of which has not yet been reached.

Karen clearly was deeply hurt, and the Community has to accept the blame corporately for what took place. On the other hand, Diane's good nature and willingness to do more than her share had also been imposed upon, so that Karen's reaction can also be questioned. Not at the point of the legitimacy of her hurt, but whether it is best for the Community as a whole for one or some members to uncomplainingly do more than their share of the housework and thus allow other members to continue, without challenge, in their irresponsible behavior. Human nature being what it is, some inequality of effort is to be expected, but Karen's contribution had made it easier for some, like Gary, to take for granted what no member in a Community of this kind should take for granted—the expectation that if I don't clean up or pull my weight, someone else will do the work.

A meeting between the principals took place, but no resolution of the conflict occurred. Gary announced his irrevocable decision to leave the Community, and no amount of pleading for some discussion could budge him. He even refused to talk about it.

In retrospect it is difficult to be just to all concerned. Gary has some justification in that he has tried at points where others have not, been faithful in attendance at meetings where others have not. But his continual abrasive manner has caused deep and unhappy feelings to arise in the girls in particular. I am convinced that Gary does not wish it to be so. He admits that his cold intellectualism is a front, and confesses willingly that he does not know how to deal with the forces that cause him to be so defensive. He has come to expect the worst from life and as a result he finds it. This has left a bitterness in him which breaks out in destructive anger against others, with a force and intensity he is quite unable to control.

But at this stage it seems that for the sake of the whole Community it is necessary for one member to leave its ranks. After a great deal of thought I have come painfully to the conclusion that it will be best for the Community and for Gary if he moves out of the house. The problem about that is, he has nowhere to go and no one willing to go with him.

In visiting the house for the first time after the events above described, I learned how profoundly it had affected other members of the Community. The shock was still apparent in the general feeling that somehow the Community had failed to act out its most firmly held convictions. Terry in particular was seriously affected because he believes so completely in what the Community is about and can offer. But everyone had realized how fragile relationships are, how much effort must be expended to keep them in good repair, and how easily much that had been painstakingly constructed can be swept away with one stroke. I sense a deeper resolve to use this experience as creatively as possible.

The meeting today, a week after the crisis, was one of the most creative we have had. To record it in cold print is impossible. We have seldom had such openness, or concern that was directed toward helping and supporting the members as they shared their hopes and fears. Sharing was, in fact, the operational word. In the case of Bruce, it involved great personal risk. But he emerged from the experience stronger and more totally confirmed by the group than he has for a long time. They silently applauded his honesty, and I do not think they will let him down. Is it that today was possible only because of what happened last Sunday when Karen left the Community? The Community classified the meeting as "ultra-berfunkling"—high praise, indeed.

Many consequences have followed from the breakup. Lisa is considering some quite radical action concerning her life. Kevin has shown himself willing to make sacrifices to be present at meetings. Graham is participating as fully as he can. Andy has been brought more completely into the group, which realizes now how much it has lost by his silence. Jack has rated the Community the priority on Sunday evenings. Karen, while not living back in the house, is present at meetings and is much wiser as a result of her action and a little more realistic about what can reasonably be expected from others. I am beginning to feel that we are strong enough as a Community to absorb much more than we have yet had thrown at us.

A strange and potentially explosive occurrence. Gary appeared at the meeting on Sunday and requested the chance to circulate to members of the Community something he had written. It is necessary to record at this point that despite what he had said almost a month ago he has not moved out of the house. He has not attended meetings, either. So it is difficult to know what he requires from the group. Is it a word that says, "Go" or one that says, "Come back"?

Gary distributed his poem entitled "Hell," and talked with the Community for forty-five minutes about his feelings. It seems that what he wanted from the Community was some understanding of his existence situation. He still intends to move out, and the Community has agreed to help him accomplish the process. The meeting succeeded in establishing a measure of sympathy and understanding, so that the break will be an amicable one. I have no grounds for changing my earlier conclusion that for Gary the Community is too threatening.

Another factor in the need to hasten Gary's leaving emerged when Lisa communicated the news to us that she had agreed with her counselor that regular counseling sessions were not helping her resolve her inability to take resolute and determined decisions. So she has stopped regular counseling sessions—a resolute action in itself. Lisa is now free to move into the house and devote time to being more completely in the Community. But that means that Karen, who is staying with Lisa, must come back also. This Karen agreed to do with some hesitation. The absence of Gary will make the difficult action of returning much easier.

MARCH

February was a month of painful learning which bore as fruit a much deeper sense of belonging. It is true in one sense that the Community had to "die" before any "resurrection" took place, but that a new style has emerged is now apparent in the increased intensity and expectancy with which members approach the meetings.

The big debate during these last meetings has been the projected move of Lisa coming into the house and, as a consequence, Karen with her. For both it involves a decision that implies considerable risk. Lisa will be entering the delicate network of relationships in the house where no one can maintain neutrality. Karen is coming back, more with a determination to lick the problem of failures in communication than with the joy of the estranged coming home. In these decisions the Community has been highly supportive. In each case, for different reasons, it is a step toward a deeper maturity.

Graham came home in time for the meeting on Sunday but indicated he was not prepared to join the group, and spent the next hour engaged in much furious activity in the basement, including the creation of a great deal of noise. No one believed he didn't want to be present, but all understood that on this occasion, because of internal stress, he couldn't hack it. And, being understood, that was accepted by the group. I think, however, that he really wanted us to come and insist that he join us, despite what he said. Otherwise, why all the noise?

At the meeting tonight Andy dropped the word, to everyone's delight, that he was to be married at the end of the month. A general chorus of delight indicated how much affection the group has for Andy and how much all shared his joy . . . an insight into the brotherliness that lives in the Community's inner life.

Graham came back this Sunday. He began in a truculent manner, found fault with people's views, upbraided them for being insensitive, and finally came off his act, admitting under careful questioning that he had been having a rough time, that the anger was really directed toward his own behavior, anger that he was projecting onto the group. And, finally, he honestly said that he had been missing the group deeply and had been hoping that the members would help him achieve the reconciliation which now he, with some relief, said he felt had been accomplished. This Community deals in Reality.

Terry and Jan have become formally engaged, the engagement symbolized in the ring that Terry proudly displayed to Community members after the meeting. It is a symbol that points to many varying and demanding facets of being adult and being responsible. Like the ring, the word "Community" is just such a symbol that also points to complex relationships of happiness, anguish, and sorrow. But the ultimate emotion is joy. Is it possible that this diamond called "Community" is a symbol of that which points to a true maturing of humanity, the growth of intimacy, the caring for others as much as for oneself?

Most of the members of the Community are carrying, or have carried, oppressive past experiences that strangle present endeavors and choke off genuine creativity in their persons. This Diary is no place to open up the many profound and deep hurts that have been shared with the group over the last weeks. It is incredible to learn what hates fester and what wounds bleed in the inner being of so many of our group. They have found a healthful release in some cases. On other occasions the attempt to achieve a cathartic release has failed. I have in mind Karen's struggle this Thursday to bring to the surface a disastrous sequence of events in her recent past. Every attempt she had made to handle the experience herself had failed. Karen knew that she needed the others to help her work through the anguish, the agony that remained. So she tried to share it. The group tried to support the endeavor and to succor her hurt, but the end was mostly failure, yet oddly a successful failure. I felt that it was a failure in which deep called to deep. The thaw may not yet have begun in that internal frozen region. But I am certain that Karen knows now that the fight is worth every cut, every blow. She has strength, drawn from her own courage and from the group's love, not to run away again, for the answer will not be found in flight but in the quiet resolute facing of the demons. None of them in any case have any real power when they are challenged.

So near and yet so far. We had a great chance to bring off a genuine celebration of the Community's existence tonight, and it failed. The meeting finished early, and it was suggested we get the guitars out and sing. Karen began with her preference for folk songs, which are generally known, but very soon Kevin had his electric guitar going, and rock was king. The chance for the whole Community to be one was destroyed by a lack of sensitivity to the general tone and experience of the group. I was angry that Kevin and Graham and Terry didn't see what they were doing, or if they did, they didn't care. So the group split up, fragmented into its parts because the needs of a few became a tyranny for the hopes of the many. So near and yet so far! I sometimes really wish that it were possible to force that responsible concern which I feel is the appropriate response to the immediate situation. But that is to magnify the problem. We must learn acceptance, and I for one can testify that it is a hard lesson to learn.

Is it possible to print with capitals the observation, A NEW PHASE HAS BEGUN? That is not a question of the typewriter's efficiency but a conviction that the Community has broken through another barrier. Two incidents illustrate. The first, that organizational demands can now be accepted without resentments against order making any scheduling or division of labor impossible. The second, a new awareness of Time.

At the meeting last evening Lisa proposed a division of labor concerning household chores. Now that she is in the house she feels strongly about the general untidiness. Not without argument and protest was the final decision made. But it was reached: Diane and Karen, the cooking and purchasing; Graham, the garbage; Kevin, the cleaning and vacuuming of the dining and living rooms; Bruce, the upper bathroom and entrance hall; Cindy, the downstairs washroom and telephone room; Lisa, the upstairs sitting room; Terry, all immediate repairs and handyman tasks. The scheme has yet to be put to the test. But it shows a growth in responsibility to each other that not all the king's horses nor all the king's men, reinforced by Diane's pleading and prodding notwithstanding, could bring off until now. It is my contention that the spirit of the Community is most manifested in the way it handles such menial chores as these. That is where cooperation and sharing finally is to find itself judged.

It was Diane's turn to be challenged tonight. Bruce with an admirable but brutal honesty (one of Bruce's greatest gifts to the Community, incidentally) took the scalpel to Diane at her most sensitive concerns. Again this is no place for the details. But the demand to face and deal with reality was unavoidably made. Diane took it in such a way that she gained the admiration of the group, and I feel that the occasion of confrontation helped Diane to experience the understanding and concern of this family. Bruce, in striking out at Diane, was striking out at himself indirectly, though no one in the group could deny his real and legitimate concern born out of his own hurts and experiences. Readers of these diary extracts can never know what incidents of such surgical penetration can mean, nor how the sense of confronting a more than contingent reality steals over the meeting. In Heidegger's term we engage in a profound Discourse, profound because more silent than spoken. The very depths of Being itself seem near to our touch in moments like this.

The kaleidoscopic series of events these last months has thrown up again and again the question of vocation.

The question elected by the group as the most urgent one is, "What can I do?" (Second place was taken by, "What kind of person can I become?") Kevin has been seized by the realization that he is squandering time and his talents to little effect. Both Bruce and Lisa, who are college dropouts, have talked about going back to school. Karen seems motivated now to seek some vocational security in education. The inevitability of time, and its lost chances, has surfaced as a concern that troubles and disturbs the group. Some of it rises from a growing realization that the Community is near its demise. We begin now to discuss the reentry process. And members are aware that we have so much to do, so much to share, so much to create. There is so little time.

We have on the walls a variety of collages that tell a story of their own. The living room is inhabited by warm thoughts and massy presences, as it sometimes is pervaded by the smell of fresh bread baking. One message is brief enough to record here:

PUSH or PULL
or
Get out of the way!

Our discussion tonight focused on the need for Community members to seek active involvement outside the life of the Community. The wheel seems to be turning full circle, so that individuals, more secure about who they are, are beginning to look for meaningful action in the city. I wrote the words below in December as a hopeful prediction of what might occur. Perhaps it has turned out much as the following predicted:

"In the long view the significance of this year in Community may not be that people were involved actively in the city's problems so much as the fact that Community members were helped to a personal maturity, a responsible enlightened vision of themselves and their charter to be 'a man for others.' And that person, striding forth to meet the world may be, in the future, a great agent for change because, in the moratorium offered by the Community, he found himself and thereby all other men."

———————

Cindy, who was absent again tonight, is not playing the game. The test is not what people say but what they do. In this case the words and the actions do not match. Cindy is a clenched fist against unrighteousness in the social scene, but in the Community she is unable to open her hand to receive or to give in significant measure. I expect the Community will ask her why she has been absent for the last three meetings despite her comments that the meetings are a priority.

———————

Gary was present at the house for supper tonight, and as seemed natural, on this occasion stayed for the meeting. But it is clear that while he is accepted by the Community as a guest, welcome for the most part, he is a guest and no longer a member of the Community. Many invisible ties now exist of which he cannot be aware.

———————

The following words, which were written in another context, seem to apply to our experience. "If life is a mere succession of unrelated and insignificant acts, with no inner telos and no strong bonds of community, then the inner sense of one's own reality tends to disappear." At its deepest level the life of the Community is assuredly a religious one, if only because we are constantly confronted with Reality. We are called by each other not only to be ourselves but to act out the truth we espouse. Demonstrably the sense of the reality of our own being fades when we can find no employment for our powers, no action congruent with our most exalted words.

One of the lessons of these last weeks is the realization that ambiguity exists in all we do. Paradoxically, that which liberates one person in the Community becomes a form of bondage to another. This is true, for example, when Kevin does his "thing," which is to play his electric guitar. Others find the volume intolerable. The same seems to be true for Cindy, who is turned off by much that is done in the Community but seemingly is inspired by the thought of what can be done outside the Community. I hesitate to fall back on folk wisdom with the observation that "one man's meat is another man's poison," but it is this constant ambiguity of response that is most difficult to balance creatively.

APRIL

The meeting this evening, the first in April, was noticeably different. Matters were raised, discussed with facility, and quickly dispatched. Often the group broke into small sections, talking about various topics. No one was "uptight." Everyone seemed at home, at ease with fellow human beings whom they respected. To employ

Bruce's term, "a mellow evening," which concluded happily with the group singing in response to Karen's guitar.

At the meeting tonight the anticipated talk with Cindy took place with the anticipated result. Perhaps every Community has someone who functions like Cindy. Cindy has said that she does not regard the meetings as important, nor the Community as a group. She disagrees with the Community's concern for people's internal needs because she wants everyone to be as socially active as she is. I think the Community has finally accepted the fact that Cindy is like this, and that no amount of pleading or arguing will change her. So they have let Cindy be present on her own terms. The problem is that although Cindy is right in asking for social involvement, she does not seem able to accept the fact that the others can't make it.

Karen has become engaged, making it three members of the Community this year. After a visit to a convention on alternative education, she returned from California, where she had been with Ray, to tell us the news. It was a happy event for us all. In reporting on the conference, Karen revealed that she sees through a view of education which simply shouts, "Give them freedom." Anarchy is no substitute for education, as we have painfully learned ourselves in a fresh way these last months.

Tonight was a bum trip. Almost so bad it was hard to believe. Everybody seemed to be experiencing a low at the same time. We were tense, irritable, defensive, nonproductive. We tried to resurrect something, but nothing came to life. The only thing that one can do on occasions like that is to walk away. I felt bad about it, as we all did, but sometimes that's the way it is. We learned that lesson at least.

What a relief! By contrast with last Sunday, tonight was as great a gathering as we have had. We talked freely about the problems of relationships, commitment to one person, the need to establish intimacy with others, marriage, and the problem of raising children without a father. Best of all, Cindy was as involved and animated as the rest.

One of the best happenings was the discussion about the problem that members of the group still have with their parents. For several that remains the key problem.

Lisa started the meeting by reading her diary of the last meeting, and her reflections on what happened subsequently. She confessed that she had expressed to the group a need for help but that it had been ignored. So time was devoted to the problem she shared. The style of honesty and openness of Lisa, I am convinced, helped others to be free. It was an occasion for rejoicing because the Community revealed the ability to minister to itself.

After struggling with the valid claims of both her fiancé and the Community, Karen decided that she would fly home and thus sever her relationship with the Community. No one was surprised that a choice had to be made, or that it was made in favor of going home. For Karen, the Community had fulfilled its function over a difficult period. Now it was time for a new beginning. Karen's leaving was the first real sign that the end is rapidly approaching. We have a consciousness of being a terminal case!

Jim Cruickshank sat in on the meeting tonight while the Community thought about its life in the light of the paper I had written. As a director of a lay training center in Canada, who works in a similar Community structure, he was competent to pass an opinion on what he saw. His judgment was that the group has pulled off a significant enterprise. So excited was he about the vitality of the discussion that he was soon participating actively himself. An index of the Community's maturity was that he felt so much at home. The members placed no barriers to Jim's full participation, although he was a stranger. That points to a security of self-awareness which is a precious and rare quality.

Diane was away at the school camp, and as far as I remember it is the first meeting she has missed. We all noticed her absence. Diane is a faithful and always reliable person whose contribution sustains and creates Community. Without her, our experience would have been considerably impoverished.

For some the breaking up of the Community is going to be a crucial occasion because they have no other place (with all the implications of that word) to go. Part of our responsibility is to work at problems of reentry.

Jack is right in raising the question, "How much can be claimed for a venture like this?" How is it to be assessed? Perhaps the real test is what Community members report concerning their own feelings. Bruce refers to the contrast between his experience before entering the Community to life in the Community as "the difference between night and day." Graham said that he felt he was coming back to life, like an arm frozen which begins to tingle painfully with a return to health. Oddly he used the death/resurrection image in talking of the change in himself! These are subjective responses, perhaps not verifiable in changed behavior. But I believe that in such cases we have genuine reporting, if only because it checks out with the perceptions of the group. That, in any case, was the level of sharing at tonight's meeting.

I have become aware this week of how much effort the maintenance of the group has required. It is not true that the group can get by without someone who is responsible to yap at their heels. In fact, often the group lacks initiative, or cannot get started of its own accord. I am disappointed that even now sometimes the task of keeping the group down to it is just as onerous as it was in the beginning.

Reduced numbers tonight, but an involved discussion about the inner meaning of sexual relations. The "new" morality gives rise to as many, or more, unresolvable dilemmas as the puritan ethic. And the double standard continues to be supported by several of the boys. What values support the new ethic? Mostly it comes off as rhetoric or rationalization, although that is also true of the "old" morality. The church's traditional arguments appear to cut no ice at all. The mood of the subculture is to reject it out of hand. In any case the arguments are of no use when they have been abandoned in practice as well as in theory.

One characteristic of the Community that is now apparent is the high level of intelligent questioning. "Formal education" has been abandoned, but a continuing hunger for explanation and meaning persists. My observation is, to modify McLuhan, that the "tube" is seldom on. Many Community members read considerably.

Bruce passed an observation of interest during a strong condemnation of the church. "They're all pro-God and antipeople. I could never tie that stuff into a life situation."

It is instructive to reflect upon a question of Terry's: "How many rules do we have?"
1. No dope in the house. (Intended seriously.)
2. No fornication on the living room couch.
Authority is very much a shared responsibility. The absence of formal rules reveals the Community's refusal to be formalized and points to the fact that, given our present state of growth, rules are unnecessary for the most part.

"Not life together, but life fractured and broken into isolatedness and solitude and loneliness: this is the reality which makes up the special kind of pathos that we meet in . . . our time."

This is what our Community has tried to overcome. As Terry said, "The great thing about this Community is that it enables people!"

MAY

How should a Community arrange its finances? There seemed to be general agreement that expecting each member to contribute his share of the rent and utilities is the most equitable arrangement. Other possibilities, such as each member contributing an agreed percentage depending on whether he was highly or poorly paid, or utilizing a common money fund with all funds being available to a member according to need, have too many problems. It has been as easy for some members to provide their share as it is to claim time for paying rent. Some would never provide their share if it was not made clear that it was expected. The lending of money to one another to pay police fines or to meet emergencies has resulted in friction because of the long delay in returning the borrowed amount. Our experience suggests that a carefully rationalized financial system is necessary to prevent real dissension. The absence of discussions on financial matters suggests that the system has worked well.

Some discussion took place tonight on the relative merits of religious terminology. Church vocabulary turns most of the Community members off, and no use of words such as redemption, estrangement, salvation, has occurred. But other words are used that carry the same weight of meaning, such as health or wholeness (salvation), acceptance (redemption), broken relationships (estrangement), celebration (worship), reflection (meditation). Getting put together, grooving with someone, hanging in, fighting it hard, being turned on, trying to make it, blowing your mind, and pronouncing life mellow are expressions that on particular occasion have described feelings and intentions of a deeply religious nature. A demythologized vocabulary is inevitable in a religionless Christianity. As a result, ordinary words come to have extraordinary symbolic force.

I spent an hour discussing the Community with a committee that is looking at the funding of the Academy. The most difficult question to answer was the question about the amount of time spent by two highly trained staff personnel with only a handful of people. Was it economical? How could such a concentration be justified? The only convincing answer would be that what we learned has produced a viable model for working with young adults, which can be used elsewhere. One questioner said, "Why can't local congregations do this?" Both Jack and I responded as one man—"They can, but they haven't." Out of our experience, however, they may be encouraged to try. If several congregations set up similar Community projects for young people, the time spent researching the Community for Urban Encounter will be well spent.

Tonight's meeting was replaced by a visit by Community members to the annual board meeting of the Academy. It was a profitable encounter. It struck me how difficult it is for dedicated people like the board members to accept what is, with its particular gains as well as failures. Many were still struggling to force the experience into the shape of what they expected or wanted to take place before the program began. A problem that is true for us all. Our expectations get in the way to the extent that we cannot be open to what actually is taking place. But like the Good, the Community "is what it is, and not another thing."

To deal decisively with the termination problem, we have decided to end the Community on June 30. After that date no formal commitment will remain. The Community as such will exist no longer. A surgical solution to a problem that has troubled us all.

George Lester, retiring president of the board, spent time with us tonight, asking sharp and penetrating questions. How different is the Community from any local congregation? Has the Community become insulated? parochial? Are the members indulgently dependent on each other? It is very easy to be defensive, we learned, about what we have done. But I think we were free enough to admit the dangers. Most of the group concluded that we had re-created a "church," but Lisa added that the basic experience was acceptance. The local congregation had not made these young people feel accepted. It was conceded, however, that what had happened in the past year could also happen in a congregational setting. Tough questions, nonetheless!

One matter that remains unresolved is the admittance or nonadmittance of new members to the group. We handled this problem badly when it arose before at the time that Gerry had asked to be admitted in February, although in retrospect the group felt that, given the circumstances at the time, we were not mature enough to act differently. But how are newcomers, strangers to a whole inner world, brought into a Community in a creative fashion? We could do it now. We couldn't handle it when the question arose in a particular form three months ago.

Catastrophe! The motor bikes were stolen this week. Terry's new bike was insured, fortunately, but Graham's older model was not. A crisis of self-image ensued. Graham had been planning to leave for New Orleans the next day on his bike for a holiday. A prolonged period of drinking and absence from the house on a "substitute" holiday followed, causing some alarm among other Community members.

Bruce used the group as a means of letting off steam tonight. The most interesting aspect was the way the group sat it out. After the storm was over, Bruce, by way of explanation, said, "When a person feels like that he needs a license to say what he thinks without caring for the effect." It is a great privilege to be able to sound off to a group of people who don't make you feel ashamed of yourself after it is over.

We planned an evening of reflection and creative expression this evening. Out of it arose one of those gentle experiences of remembering what has been done and what we have learned. Best of all, Graham was back, "clothed and in his right mind." There was no one more anxious than he to communicate how he felt about the past months. It was far from an occasion of mutual admiration, because we have grown to understand how each of us combines elements both lovable and hateful in nature. But we have the capacity now to live with each other in an accepting way. That is a kind of strength in itself.

Tonight Andy called in with his wife, whom most of us had not met. They joined in the gathering with ease and acceptance. Andy has promised to share his reflections with us at a later time. It was good to have him back. Later on Gary called in for a few moments, so that we had a brief reunion of a sort for half an hour before the meeting broke up.

Diane and Kevin shared with us what must be almost a universal human experience. Diane has at last accepted that a long-standing relationship with Doug will develop no further. Kevin, who has had an intense relationship with Meg, realizes that the friendship is disintegrating, and he knows that for him this is the worst thing he can have happen to him just now. Each of them, in their different ways, talked about the bitter taste of rejection, and about the fear of loneliness the breakup has caused. The response of the group indicated that they understood all too well what was being said. At the end of the session one of the girls offered the opinion that talking about it does no good, but Kevin disagreed. He felt more able to assess what was happening to him, more objective about it, and less tense. It reinforces my conviction that openness and the ability to share where you are with a group of peers you can trust are crucial needs of this age group and a proper function of Community.

We now have two additional people living in the house. They are to participate in the Academy's summer program, and one of them, Barbara, is planning to join the next Community which forms in September. It is of interest to notice how they do not gather the full import of what is said, often because they simply respond to the words. But for the members of the Community the words are only a part of the total communication. We know each other so well that how it is said, or when it is said, or why it is said, becomes an important element in the hearing of what is said. The exchange with the newcomers will enrich our life considerably, and I venture to suggest they will learn quickly that facility with words is not enough to live in this Community.

JUNE

The discussion began with Terry in what was an evening of severe testing for many. With the wedding only a matter of weeks away, he and Jan are experiencing the doubts and uncertainties, which inevitably arise, with peculiar intensity. The group wrestled with Terry until he finally came to the point where he saw clearly what action could be taken. His relief at being able to grasp some positive direction was obvious.

Diane followed with a frank explanation about where she was, now that there seemed little chance that her expectations would materialize in relation to Doug. As Bruce listened he came to the realization that all his life he had feared rejection. A long discussion ensued, with Bruce being told that the power to "let being be" was as great as the continual assaults upon problems with the intention of destroying them once and for all. The latter procedure, Bruce admitted, had failed. So the group offered some other images for his consideration—not pulling yourself up by your bootstraps but a quiet, trustful response, like floating in a pool. Bruce avowed that he was digging it.

At this juncture Jenny, a visting house member, said she wanted the chance to talk something out. Most of it revolved around a relationship with Kevin that she felt had been betrayed. Kevin sat with his head bowed. So Jenny was told to address him directly, which, with admirable courage, she did. Jenny felt sexually used and deceived. Kevin heard straight words about the feeling of being hurt because no genuine concern existed in the other. He took it manfully. In response he admitted he had no defense for his actions. But then he went on to tell the group that in a talk with Meg over the weekend he discovered she had been sleeping with his best friend. The traumatic impact of this revelation was still with him. It seemed that all his pigeons were coming home to roost at the same time. He was suffering deeply.

The meeting finally ended close to midnight, but not before Graham had asked if he could have time at the next gathering to talk about what he could do to face up to the loss of the group's support at the end of the month when the Community breaks up. So the agenda for the next meeting seems set.

Several rules of thumb operate in the group when a meeting gets down to basics, as it did this meeting. The first is that if a person wants help, he must ask for it. When he has asked for it the group then suspends other concerns to deal exclusively with that person's problem. He is open to the group's support or criticism and must recognize that the group has the right to press for explanation. Another understanding is that the person in question has the power to suspend the conversation at any time. But the group will not change the subject until the person who asked for help releases the group by saying he is satisfied or has had enough. The newcomers have been advised of these local rules. And no one will explain to the group the problem of another member. Each member must tell his own story, for the risk of sharing oneself is an indispensable element in the healing process.

Graham talked openly tonight about the choice he now sees before him. The playboy existence he has found sterile. In the Community he has learned self-respect and has gathered inner resources to cope with his problems. But he is not yet prepared to choose one direction, because he wants the best of both worlds. His greatest fear is that when the Community breaks up he will crumple under outside pressure. He finds himself over an abyss. He fears the nothingness, the terror, the threat of nonbeing. He knows he must choose his future and his choice literally means life or death, because the drug route spells destruction for him.

The Community responded by suggesting that perhaps he had already made his decision, although he does not know it. He is now only trying to live with the consequences. Graham agreed that he was growing up. It was a most moving and powerful testimony to the Community's love and influence. Graham has begun, with a courage one can only wonder at, a long, difficult journey to the sun.

The heat of the Chicago summer beat us tonight. It was far too hot for us to concentrate, so we sat on the stoop outside and chatted until the hour was late. But there was something in that occasion of the memory of childhood, of the family sitting together in the cool of the evening before the night fell and the world grew cruel.

Jenny has soaked up the Community's ready acceptance and has begun to exploit it by coy and at times superficial behavior. Tonight the Community played back to her their feeling that she was not being herself. What was remarkable about this incident was the recognition that every member began his life in the Community with the same self-protective behavior. For us it has long since been unnecessary to play roles with each other. We have gratefully dropped our masks and learned to accept ourselves and others as we are. Jenny was told either to work on something worthwhile if she wanted the group's attention or to stop wasting the time of the meeting. "Push or pull or get out of the way!" She responded with a mixture of hurt and genuineness that revealed she had understood what had been said to her in love. It is a road we have all traveled this year.

Graham, for the first time since he can remember, had a day about which he could rejoice. He was on top of the world. His boss had praised him. He was seeing things straight for the first time in his life. So when the meeting began, in high good spirits, he made comments and jokes right and left. But one, which had no malicious intent, cut Bruce to the raw. He came back like a cornered wildcat.

In what followed, Graham was brought to tears. He had been vulnerable and, unsuspecting of any attack, was mortally wounded. Out of his misery he struggled in a bewildered fashion to comprehend what had happened to his perfect day. The wretchedness of his life came out. We saw the crippling, brutalizing forces that had shaped his world. His cry for human understanding, love, and comfort was well-nigh unbearable. Bruce was stricken by the realization of what he had done. He saw how he had forced upon Graham a conclusion that could only cause Graham more self-doubt and pain. Massive guilt overwhelmed him, although he has lived through much the same story as Graham has.

In these moments the Community was truly itself. The members sat, listened, supported, loved, comforted, judged, suffered, and rejoiced with each of the combatants until the wounds were healed and peace returned. At the end, Bruce, out of his new understanding, cried: "Thank God for these people! Thank God for the Community!" I might have hoped at times for a happy, jovial ending to our life together, but that is a fantasy.

Tonight was real, in the only way that matters, in the midst of the greatness and wretchedness of the human condition. We have fought and we are victors. We need no greater knowledge than that.

It was interesting to read a remark of Toynbee's and translate it into our experience. Our society has "substituted the art of speaking for the art of living." At its best the Community forced people to reject the former and led them to consider the latter. The art of living does seem to be a lost art among us.

When the Community concludes, it will be necessary for many of its members to set up alternative support systems. Diane mentioned tonight that she had noticed a tendency in herself to fall back into familiar and noncreative ways of responding. Like an old boxer springing to the ready position at the ringing of a bell, many are tempted to adopt familiar poses that no longer relate to the reality they see. Former methods of coping with internal stress are seen to be inadequate, so we talked at length with Bruce, Graham, Terry, Diane, and Barbara, who was present, about alternate support systems available to them. An intelligent handling of the Community's breakup includes such an exercise and needs to be self-consciously a part of the preparation for leaving the house.

Upon reflection, Langdon Gilkey's comment in *Shantung Compound* appears to be the most apposite to what has happened. "For no program in the life of a commu-

nity is really just if that program cannot be enacted."
That seems to me now to be unanswerable.

Lisa called on the Community for help tonight. The
readiness of the response and its warm, concerned nature
were the real gifts of the occasion. We will all miss the
feeling of being surrounded by people who care for us.
There are only three meeting nights left.

The group discussed also how dependent they were
on my leadership at times, and yet how often they had
taken the initiative and handled their own problems.
What seemed to gain general assent was the conclusion
that if a leader appears competent and gives a feeling of
security to others, they will attempt things for themselves. If they feel, however, that the leader does not
understand what is happening, or that they cannot respect him, then the group uncertainty immobilizes its
energies. Being free yourself is an essential ingredient to
freeing others to be themselves.

A most powerful expression of our life together is con-
veyed in the words of a new banner, made by Diane,
hanging in the living room: YOUR LIVES HAVE PENE-
TRATED MY DARKNESS.

Our last meeting was a non-happening. It is fair to say
that we didn't have a final meeting. A number of factors
combined to make the gathering an unproductive experience, the strongest being the group's awareness that
this was the last time we would meet as a Community.

It was the end of a family experience that could never be repeated. That was the real sadness. It was time to begin new tasks, to set out again on the next stage without trusted comrades.

———

All that remains for us as a group is the celebration on Saturday night. The lease expires three days later. Then we shall be scattered to all corners, as we were before the Community drew us together. That will be good-by in a final sense. One thinks of Shakespeare's words:

> Whether we shall meet again I know not,
> Therefore our everlasting farewell take.
> . . . .
> If we do meet again, why, we shall smile;
> If not, why then, this parting was well made.

III

REFLECTIONS
UPON AN ODYSSEY

TERRY WAS HUNCHED FORWARD in the big chair in the corner. His Peace medallion swung slowly on its leather chain as he clenched his hands and searched for words. They came slowly, stumblingly, as he shared with the group the pain he was experiencing. The others listened intently. Diane lay on the floor, head propped on her elbows. Lisa and Graham shared the spare mattress that doubled as a living room couch. Bruce, his feet stretched out over the coffee table, sat silently in the other corner. Kevin was buried in a large armchair. Barbara, eyes bright with interest, sat beside him.

As had occurred on many occasions, the Community began slowly to pull together the various pieces of the situation. Terry was asked to clarify why he had acted one way and not another. The group investigated the problem Terry had presented until the issue began to emerge. Lisa was comforting, offering explanations for Jan's reaction. At a particularly difficult point Barbara was asked to role-play Jan's response, and Terry began to put into words what he had been unable to say the weekend before when the fight began.

Gradually the fear of being rejected by Jan emerged.

Terry began to reveal signs of relief as he understood the situation more clearly. Positive suggestions were made. Hard judgments were passed. Predictions were laughingly made of the outcome of the action proposed. With a cry Terry sank back into the cushions. "I feel better now. I think I see what I can do." One of the members suggested that Terry receive a group hug, and amid much laughter and sharing he was hugged by the whole group.

The tension was broken. Someone went to the kitchen for coffee, others lighted cigarettes. Inconsequential chatter broke out. Slowly the noise abated, people settled down once more. Then Diane lifted her head and began to talk about how Terry's fear of rejection spoke to her own. The meeting moved into another moment of sharing. This evening was typical of many other such evenings. The Community was at work. Here, in mutual support and exploration, members of the group began to test themselves, try new ideas, confess failure, and seek guidance and support.

On this occasion Diane was followed by Bruce and Kevin who also wanted to deal with "unfinished business." Finally, as midnight struck, the meeting broke up after a five-hour session. No one could really assess what had happened that evening. Nor could they the many meeting nights in the last nine months when the same sharing of their inner life occurred. But they had a word for it They called it "berfunkling." What does it mean to live in such a Community? How do the members view their life together? Do changes occur? In answer to these questions the members of the Community can speak for themselves.

GARY   Gary left the Community after five months. He found that living in close contact with the others demanded changes in behavior he was not prepared to make. The parting was friendly, however, and after leaving the house, Gary came back one evening to share the following poem with us:

HELL

The Sun has risen.
The Sun has set.
And here I sit staring out from within my prison
—my prison without bars—

The past is past.
The past is present.
The past is the future.
Yet I live
With my mind bound with imaginary chains.
All this I have been forced to choose.
Forced to deny my freedom, my existence,
My right to create my own essence.

And who is to blame?
There they are—see them—
The others—those people.
They are the culprits who have damned me.
See them love and hate,
Weep and laugh,
Live and die,
Because of the others I have chosen my hell
—my hell on earth—

The divorce, the child,
The lover, the environment.
To their values I pay homage
And reject responsibility.

My prison protects me.
There I am safe.
No need to risk,
No need to create my existence.
No need to seek freedom
—for myself or others—
So it is and so shall it be
A coward now—a coward forever.

And when I die
The Sun will rise and the Sun will set.
And here I'll sit staring out from within my prison
—my prison without bars—

He explained: "What I am trying to say is that I feel the outside world or certain things have happened to me. I was free to respond in any way, but I have chosen to exclude myself from that world—in my own personal hell rather than the external hell. I want it to be different, but that's not the way it's going to be."

When asked why he wrote the poem and shared it with the Community, he was equally honest.

"I guess maybe also it was mine and not a creature of some other part of society. The fact that whatever it was about, it was some way part of me. . . . What I was most seeking was some appreciation of the hassles I was going through."

JANE   Other members shared with Gary a disappointment with the Community. Jane, who left the Community before Gary, communicated her state of mind this way:

"When I left I was upset because I couldn't talk in groups. I have many hassles and problems on my mind. I cannot make any commitment or statement—my mind is really messed up."

CINDY   Cindy, who remained in the Community, also felt disappointed.

"I expected an Action-Reflection group, one year in Chicago involved in dialogue, community work, and reading in order to learn about, evaluate, and participate in social action.

"The Community became a year of personal introspection among the Community members. This is good. But for me it was not enough. Interpersonal relationships are very important to me. Very. But they are not enough to keep me alive and well in a program that does not excite me to social action.

"I still believe that Community is good, very good, but not this Community. Not for me. Not this time. Right now I want to consider why this Community didn't work for me. Or is it why didn't I work for this Community? I really don't know."

LISA   Lisa, however, found in the Community what she had been seeking.

"The most rewarding experience for me was the total acceptance. When I first joined the Community in October, I felt emotionally inhibited. I had difficulty expressing what I was feeling."

What that meant can best be gathered in an incident Lisa regarded as important for her.

"At this time I was not living in the house, but rather with a girl friend in an apartment about six blocks away. One particular evening before a Community meeting, Christine, my roommate, and I had been talking about what she felt was my lack of responsiveness to her. It was as though I was simply living in the same apartment with her but never really 'there,' not sharing nor seemingly wishing to share. My reaction was one of confusion. I didn't know what she meant.

"That particular evening at the Community we dealt with a problem of Cindy's and her relationship to the members of the house. As I sat and listened I realized they were calling on Cindy to be responsive, just as Christine had called on me. I suddenly knew what Christine had been talking about. Cindy was where I had been only a couple of hours before, unresponsive, confused, and feeling pressed for something she didn't really understand or feel. Both for her and for myself I became upset and unhappy with my inability to say what I felt.

"Following the meeting we all walked down to the lake and then returned to the house. I felt that no one had realized or seemed to notice how really upset I was. Then Kevin turned and said, 'Where does it hurt?'

"So the whole group sat down and listened to me talk —about Christine and her hassle with me, about my frustration with my parents and our lack of communication, about my general feeling of neither hearing others nor being heard, about my inability to express my feelings. Terry, Graham, and Kevin, in particular, prodded me to talk, forced me to admit my anger with them, then when I let it out, affirmed me as a person.

"It is one of the most frightening and at the same time most rewarding experiences possible to make yourself vulnerable and to close your eyes in fear of the awful possibilities and to open them to find yourself safely and surely supported by friends. While I will never find another experience to match this year in the Community, I know now what it is to share, to trust, to need and be needed by others."

When Lisa was asked to comment on the year, she wrote:

"Living in Community is like living with the door open. The greatest gift from the Community has been the knowledge that I matter. Listening to others when they needed to talk, I have found myself sharing a strength I had not been aware of. And when the hurt in me becomes overwhelming I can trust in their being for me—to listen, to hold me, to convince me that I need not fear. . . . Because of the Community I began to feel a completeness about myself."

KEVIN   Kevin also, in his unique way, responded positively to life in the Community. An illustration of the other members' tolerance was that no one actually wrapped Kevin's electric guitar around his ears, although a neighbor did throw a brick through the window on one occasion when the noise was extreme. The Community members knew how much the guitar meant to him. His heroes were easily discovered. Taped to the large mirror in the living room was a photograph of George Harrison. Underneath were the words: "This is George Harrison. *HE* can play guitar." A more negative identification existed with a guitarist, Mike Bloomfield. An abstract collage Kevin had made hung on the living room wall with words from Bloomfield: "What the hell—How much do we know?"

"What the hell—How much do we know?" was a philosophy that Kevin found peculiarly persuasive. But he found in the Community that some things can be known and communicated with surprising force and penetration. As he later admitted:

"The point is that philosophers never tell you to do anything but open your eyes, never give any instructions. It's like tapping you on the shoulder when you are asleep. That doesn't say, 'Get up and wash your face.'"

Later he was to urge Terry:

"If you believe something, you've got to force it on other people. Identity is *your values*."

What, then, did Kevin gain from the Community? He had come to understand, he said, "A Rose of Obviously Superior Quality."

"A boy of six was headed home from school one afternoon when he chanced upon a rose of obviously superior quality. Thinking it would be a happy gift for his mother, he plucked it and proceeded homeward. As he walked he inspected the rose and wondered what gave this particular one its obviously superior quality. Something deep within, no doubt. He pulled off a petal for a closer look. Then a leaf . . . another petal. Shortly he found himself holding the pieces of a no longer superior rose. 'Perhaps my mother will know what's wrong,' he said.

"Here the story ends. In the case of our Community we were looking for something intangible. I am sure this caused us to lose it more than once. But I consider further. I am inclined to believe that a botanist must have a hard time seeing the obviously superior quality of a rose. On the other hand, the botanist has acquired the capacity of breeding a more beautiful rose. He needs a special strength to retain his humanity in the face of his knowledge.

"The past year has made botanists of us all!"

TERRY   Terry had few words of reflection but considerable advice.

"To try to record all the things, the deep things, that happened to people on paper is a real injustice. I don't think words exist that could describe me now as compared to me pre-Community. I like the word 'together,' though. I feel more together, the people here feel together, and there is a together sort of feeling about the whole place."

Advice was freely available from Terry, who drew up the following:

DO'S AND DON'TS FOR COMMUNITY

DO'S	DON'TS
1. Have a member who likes to shop and cook and will do it.	1. Wear somebody else's shirt without asking!
2. Buy locks so that nothing gets stolen.	2. Destroy somebody's record collection.
3. Hug each other individually.	3. Push dope.
4. Hug each other collectively.	4. Work the 4:00 to midnight shift.

DO'S	DON'TS
5. Stay up till 4:00 shooting the bull.	5. Play your electric guitar very loudly in the middle of the night (results in a brick coming through the window!).
6. Carry enough cigarettes so other smokers can bum from you.	6. Play a record player through a guitar amplifier very loudly.
7. Put up something that belongs to you in the living room.	7. Take any bull from your adult advisers (if you have any, or if such animals exist at all).
8. Hook the doors while showering. Beware of flying cold water.	8. Spend any more than 5 percent of your waking hours in your room.
9. Go to Sir Whoopee's and the beach together in a convertible.	9. Leave the kitchen messy.
10. Take out the garbage.	10. Complain about the food if you don't wash dishes.
11. Have one large table that everybody can sit around.	11. Be late in paying your rent.
12. Listen!	12. Drink somebody else's beer.
13. Share!	13. Complain about burned out light bulbs. Change them!
14. Make a whole pot of tea, not one cup.	14. Be afraid.

DO'S	DON'TS
15. Pay your bills.	15. Break all of somebody's three for $1 wine glasses.
16. Make somebody listen.	16. Lie.
17. Have pillows.	17. Sell out.
18. Read what you write.	18. Pull a *coup d'état*.
19. Eat.	19. Become intrigued with your own voice.
20. CELEBRATE LIFE HARD!	20. CELEBRATE LIFE TOO LONG!

DIANE   Diane, who gave the Community much of its stability, found that in return the group enlarged her horizons immeasurably. What that meant can be gathered from a letter she wrote to a friend in the early months of the Community's life but never sent.

"If superstability was my complaint—which it seems to have been as I look back on last year's dilemma and decision-making period—then *that* I've succeeded in escaping. One thing my life is *not* at present is stable—and that seems to apply to all facets of it!

"The relationships within the Community are continually changing, developing, being reshaped or renewed, exploding and needing to be re-created, or subtly shifting in depth or mood. At the moment there are seven of us living in the big, old deparsoned parsonage that we've rented for the year as our Community Center and Home: three guys and four girls. That's varied greatly at times, with two people leaving and dropping out of Community for Urban Encounter because they did not like the direction in which it was going.

"The year has been a learning experience in hundreds

of ways for me. The basic learning is: You can live with, learn to understand and love, grow and share with people with whom you seem at first to have nothing in common; people whose life-styles and personal standards seem to be totally opposed to your own—you *can*, if you are committed together to a common goal and all willing to work toward that goal.

"My idealism, built in my sheltered environment, reinforced through the years by Young Adults, the church, college, teaching in the suburbs, etc., is meeting the cold test of reality in the city. All the questions that were answered—theoretically—years ago have to be reconsidered as they become viable alternatives, or even as you live with people who have answered them differently: the questions of 'free love,' cohabiting vs. marriage, bribing policemen, prosecuting a thief, marijuana, LSD, drug pushers, making room for the stranger at our gates, the experimental church vs. 'God is dead' or never was, new schools, alternatives in education, rock? blues? folk?, fighting the 'system' . . . and all the other 'storybook questions' that become very real as you live with them—whether you're facing them yourself or responding to someone who is dealing with them."

When asked to define "berfunkling," Diane contributed the following:

BERFUNKLING

B eing open—being honest—being concerned—
E veryone shares of himself.
R espect for each other grows as we share,
F or we reach unaccustomed depths in

U nderstanding why people are as they are.
N ew communication skills are truly the
K ey to understanding and clearer perception—
L istening with love, as others risk in Trust.
I is no longer the most important word.
N othing that's important to You is unimportant
     as we
G row in self-perception and ability to give of
     ourselves through encounter with others.

What Diane was seeking she found in considerable measure.

"I had a need to communicate. And to find also a hope worth communicating, with people you can celebrate joys with as well as share problems. The value of the Community has been to help each one of us to become a responsible individual who can make value judgments."

BRUCE   Bruce often helped other members understand what the Community demanded.

"There is a thin line between individual integrity and group integrity. Adjustments have to be made. Compromise is inevitable. But what we are after is a cognizance of each other's feelings. And in that you have to pay the cost. Responsible action means that you have to hurt someone."

For Bruce, generalizations or vagueness were anathema. People had to say exactly what they meant and why. On this matter the practice of the Christian faith came under his condemnation.

"How can you discover what power is if you keep generalizing? I wonder about the Christian religion. Power is when you make a difference, and I don't see any difference."

The Community gave Bruce the kind of support that he needed. For him, being in the Community, when compared with his world before, was the difference between night and day.

"For me, I feel far more committed to people. It may sound strange, but I feel bewildered by a lot of things. And it's not a matter of organization. For what the Community is for me, organization and disorganization don't apply."

ANDY   Andy entered the Community seeking a sympathetic group of people who would understand his work in a community organization. But he never sought an intellectual response.

"The rational level is no answer. And that's the reaction I have come to expect, even from this group at times."

Andy had one important question which he wrestled with himself and forced the Community to wrestle with also.

"Do you have a common sense of what it means to be human?"

He was interested in creating an alternative life-style that he could believe in and affirm. The practice of the group to confront each member and ask him what he meant was very helpful to Andy. To be taken seriously as a developing human being enabled Andy to work out many conflicts that he had.

For him, American life had patterns in which, against his will, he was forced to act. By contrast the Community offered the chance for a group of people to create their own patterns. The real joy for Andy was the chance to participate from the beginning in the attempt to build an alternate life-style. In his own words, "The celebration of a creative life-style is the only way to break out of the cycle of American un-life." He was dedicated to learning what it is like to be free, and thereby to free others. That quest was Andy's gift to the Community.

GRAHAM   The Community provided Graham with a concerned and available peer group which he had never experienced before. He fought the influence of the others until their acceptance forced him to respond positively. What was most significant about this caring was that, in giving Graham support, it inhibited his ability to find escape in his usual activities.

As he confessed one night:

"Drugs are supposed to release you. I would take 'hash,' 'tea,' 'acid,' or get drunk for that release. When I had a bad trip on acid I couldn't believe it. [Graham was referring at this point to three days spent in the hospital as the result of drugs taken at Christmas when he was alone in the house.] I get bitching on drugs now. A change has taken place, because before my desire was unfulfilled by other people. It's a change I haven't examined. I never bum on LSD, or when I did last time I didn't believe it. I bummed the next time also, which shows a change. It comes on you heavy. I'm presented with a problem and I have no answer. Drugs and booze don't make it for me anymore. Man, I don't get there with either."

Later, he was able to say:

"This Community has been a success, we have managed to establish trust. It's all boiled down to trust."

But perhaps the most revealing insight of the importance of the Community to Graham is the way he began a reflection on his experience. "*My* Community." He was, at least for a time, "home."

"My community is a grindstone. I am a diamond in the rawest form, needing to be cut and polished. As a diamond is ground with abrasive materials, I have been ground by the Community to reveal to the world what I am and can be. Grinding a diamond causes heat, and grinding a person causes pain, but when the pain is over no scar is left. In its stead is the first facet of a precious stone, and one less pain to be felt. Time and time again the wheel is applied. The result, a shower of pain, anger, and the beginnings of self-awareness. Admire a diamond and respect yourself. I am a diamond— look at me!"

KAREN   Karen suffered as much as Graham from her experience in the Community. She arrived in the Community desperate for self-understanding, unsure of herself, anxious to be loved and to give love. The early period with its tensions and uncertainties, its anger, frustration, and even spite, caused her anxiety to deepen. In particular she was completely dispossessed by the demand of some of the members that involvement in the city was mandatory. Karen responded in this way:

"How about an experiment in radical living? At the roots of our human joys and problems? An attempt to develop the quality of relationships that mean living, not surviving. If in one year we could struggle through this together, discovering together, unfolding and deepening and making sense out of our experiences as individuals and as a group, sharing the feelings and values that determine our life-styles, just for once to be people and everything that means. If we could say, 'Fork your system and antisystem, this is the way to LIVE, and if you share our passion to be human, come with us.'

"We are so unaware of our possibilities. We are wasting our chances to understand and learn from each other. The real Community that we sometimes have is such a delicate and fragile thing; it has been killed too many times, it has been stomped on by our harshness, our turning each other off, our concern for pride and protection. But it keeps coming back when we are not afraid to be real, to unmask our certainty, or when we share our searching, and sometimes finding.

"I really think this is the only way to go—not to come and attempt to destroy what is decaying and oppressive, necessitating violence, manipulating and destroying people's integrity—to say damn all that and build what you can believe in. This is something that has to be built consciously into our lives together, into every response we make to each other. I know most of you don't share these feelings, but it is where I am. Please take it as *the* most important thing to me."

Later, when Karen had become engaged and flown home, she was able to be objective about what had happened.

"I think the results of our initial crisis showed a lot about what really concerns us deep down, even if we couldn't express it in a positive way. We couldn't become involved in the outside community of Chicago at that point—we weren't ready, we had skipped important phases of our development. Slowly and painfully most (never all) of us realized that what was inside us—ourselves and our relationships as a Community—was of most vital importance. Maybe most of us had struggled through 'Who am I?' but the whole thing needed to be redefined when 'I' was in such close contact with so many 'Thou's.' The Community rejected rhetoric—you had to be in your actions what you were in your head. This is reality—not an isolated do-your-own-thing but identity-in-community, the essential thing not you or me but the relationship.

"There are so many things I learned about myself and about people, things that probably haven't begun to affect me yet because I think we were able to cut through the conventions and defenses we had been forced to develop, and respond with honesty and warmth and trust and support to the human beings that we discovered. It is this kind of relationship, this community of trust and growth, that holds all the meaning I can see in life, and it has been lost in our society. . . . 'Once there was a way to get back home.' Community is home. Only when we were secure in that could we attempt to relate to organizations for change in the city. And I don't think any of us will leave without the awareness that we have experienced the very inside of life: we have understood and celebrated what is Now."

The day Karen left the Community a note was found attached to the refrigerator door:

be learning

surely

we must

mistake

. . . . With every

Thank you fire. Thank you for my warm heart.
Love always,

Karen

JIM   Jim, dean of the Lay Academy, who
participated in the enterprise from the beginning, shared
with the Community a feeling of accomplishment.

"I would affirm that significant enabling has in fact
taken place. There is both a weakness and a strength in
such a testimony. It lacks the empirical accompaniment
of long-haul acts. But then any means we employed
would lack these at this stage. The strength of the testimony is that it is verified by the Community members.
It is their story, not our wish projection.

"In a deep sense, to take one example, the testimony of
Cindy, that despite her disappointment with the final
shape the Community took, it has helped her to stand up
for her decisions, might mean more than any set of conclusions we may have led her to accept. I believe it does.

"The implications of the year are clear. In addition to
creating new models and contexts for skill acquisition
and theological clarity in the job of urban reformation,
we must take the carrier of the skills and clarity seriously. Experiments such as these provide new models
and contexts for personal growth and affirmation that
can bring fresh possibilities to the local congregation."
DENHAM   In the early months of the Community's
life as it struggled to survive, both Jim and I felt the
despair of ever bringing order out of the apparent primal
chaos. It was a rough time. After one particularly stormy

meeting I wrote the following poem out of frustration
and helplessness, and shared it with the Community.

I TRY TO TELL THEM

i try to tell them that
This life offers few second chances
and that Rainbow gold is never found.
If we cannot link hands in this moment
we almost certainly
will not have another quite like it,
Cocoon-full of butterfly possibilities
Which die stillborn
For Summer warmth that never seems to come.

i try to listen for that
which screams through our long Silences
but all that comes is the buzz
of minor irritations that
We must constantly swat at
until wearied we go home to
Our very own color.

i try to feel that nameless dread
of being left alone
Or totally ignored
Like the old man who shared his wine
with me, Quoted poetry
and sat daily on the park bench
Opposite the place where his ex-wife lived.
Love may never grow cold but it can become lonely
Waiting.
But are we waiting? i try to feel that.

Perhaps i should fly to Florida
it's warm there
and the windy city can give up its sheets of
Daily News blown from ghetto grays
and gold coast slums, unread
although the inch high Banner warns
"We are killing ourselves"
and all my important somethings are nothing.
Perhaps i should fly to the sun.

But God it's like Malnutrition
to eat cardboard words in Lonely Halls
Turn on the tapes and let me hear
Sergeant Pepper's Band.
An awful lot of people listening
I hear the rustle of their breathing
But my earmuffs distort the sound.
The music swings but no one dances.
The piper plays his tune, we do not follow.
Perhaps God they have never seen the Sun
there in the cave.
Could that be it?

I try to tell them that
it will soon be time to move on
and i try to listen so that
i may not miss the whispered why
i try to feel the new birth begin
perhaps for joy, a deeds leap in the grass.
Or can it be that i am in the wrong house
Guest at a party of unknown people
Who plan one day to fly to Florida—
Together.
Could that be it?

But the early period of crisis was conquered, and the Community grew to become to us all a precious thing. What then was learned?

I grew to see clearly that finally there is no distinction between personal and social transformation. They feed into each other, and this year's search for personal integration has its authentic social consequences.

I learned also how far the institutional church is from young people like the Community members, and how open they are to affirming its essential proclamation once it is stripped of its traditional wrappings and unholy piety. I understand also why young people crave for an accepting fellowship and how little we grasp the true essence of "community" in the modern world.

But above all I was brought into the intimate, living struggles of people I grew to love, so that our essential humanness became transparent and something of the mystery of our existence was disclosed. It is that gift of trust and affection which has enriched my own life immeasurably. It has cast out fear. And I learned to believe afresh that working in our midst is that power which still can make men whole.

LIVING IN A COMMUNITY IS:

Having a shoulder to cry on (a multiple one).

Knowing you'll be missed if you're missing.

Listening to people you care about, with people you care about.

Walking barefoot through Old Town for an ice-cream cone.

Being stabbed where it hurts because somebody cares.

Picking up the pieces and helping to put them together when somebody falls or slips.

Learning what you're really like, as you see how others see you.

Being challenged to share your convictions, and to justify them.

Big bear hugs.

Lending and borrowing.

Doing new things with new people.

Tripping over everybody and their belongings.

Leaning on others—and not only when your ankle's not working!

A time of Becoming . . .

IV

EDUCATIONAL CONCERNS

Some Guidelines for Community Living

WIDESPREAD INTEREST EXISTS at the present time in experiments of communal living, and a multitude of attempts are being made to establish helpful communities of concerned people. Some people prefer to call their venture a "commune"; others, an "order"; some a "family." It is difficult to decide whether these are different names for the same kind of experience or whether they differ at fundamental points.

Each community is different in matters of detail from every other simply because of the infinite variety of human goals, expectations, individual behavior, and local situations. But it is possible to isolate some general elements that might serve as a guide to those interested in beginning a communal experience. In each case the way the Community for Urban Encounter responded to the issue will be outlined. Obviously other ways of dealing with these matters exist. But some consideration of the following concerns appears inevitable whatever the decisions taken by individual groups.

1. *Conflict.* Every Community will experience conflict. The test is whether members can learn to handle conflict creatively. In some cases it may result in a member or members leaving the project, as happened with Jane and Gary. Yet, it was out of the explosive situation between Gary and Karen that the Community entered the most productive phase of its existence. As a general rule, therefore, members were encouraged to deal openly in the meetings with their anger and frustration toward other members. We gradually learned not to be too defensive when attacked, to state honestly how we felt, and to work toward reconciliation even in the midst of pain and humiliation. As a result a positive direction was possible in conflict situations because the experience of Community affection and well-being was prized so highly. It was not an unambiguous success, as Cindy would testify, but the climate of concern enabled members to handle tense emotional crises and through them to grow in personal maturity.

2. *A Shared Environment.* Not only did the house provide a common place of meeting available to all, it also thrust people into the inner depths of sharing themselves. The problem of individual privacy and communal responsibility was thereby sharply raised. After several months it was accepted that each member had the right to retire to his room for moments of solitude without being bothered. Areas of withdrawal were as important as areas of involvement.

A continuing difficulty with the communal areas was created by the influx of the friends of one or two members who prevented other community members from watching television, preparing lessons, or engaging in general social activities. Normally permission was requested from other members to bring in friends for a party or a gathering before the event, but this was not always possible. To some it may appear as if more is to be lost than gained from sharing the same living quarters, but the result of this kind of situation was an awareness of the need to compromise, to make personal sacrifices, and to consider the demands of others. Out of the dynamic that followed from the common environment much of the learning dimension of the experience resulted.

3. *Finance.* Another essential concern is a carefully rationalized financial system clearly understood and accepted by all members. Perhaps the Community was not strictly a commune because it did not share all its goods in common. Each member was responsible for a monthly contribution, which was an equal share of rent, utilities, and food costs. Experience revealed that even with this clear understanding some members were slow in fulfilling their financial obligations. When a special case of hardship arose some concessions were made, but mostly each member was expected to be prompt in meeting his financial commitments. On one occasion it was necessary to discuss a member's delinquency with him in one weekly gathering where the matter was quickly and amicably resolved.

Other ways of organizing finance exist, such as a common sharing of all funds, or a proportional contribution according to income earned. For the Community's part the members decided on a system that required an equal effort from all. It worked surprisingly well, so that a potential source of destructive conflict was avoided.

4. *An Acceptable Minimum Commitment.* When members enter into Community they need to be aware of what is required of them, in general terms. Financial obligation is one concern. Another may relate to duties necessary for the proper functioning of the Community house. In the case of the Community for Urban Encounter it also involved being present at two gatherings a week, attendance at which all recognized as a demonstration of each person's willingness to participate in the Community's life.

When Jane and then Cindy began to be absent from meetings for reasons that were vague, it became apparent that a basic disagreement existed concerning the functioning of the Community. Jane left shortly after. Cindy remained and made an effort to participate, although it proved unfruitful for her. But at least a norm existed against which involvement could be tested. The absence of any criteria would have left the Community unable to decide what responsible action involved.

5. *Basic Disagreements.* A generally understood position on matters of essential disagreement is also necessary. The diverse nature of the Community's personnel produced many areas of fundamental disagreement. These included sexual behavior, the use of drugs, visitors to the house, invasion of privacy, the eating of food in the refrigerator, or the sharing of door keys with non-Community members. The latter practice was blamed for the two robberies that the Community experienced. On both occasions the loss of property was only moderate, but the rise of insecurity among Community members was great.

Whatever the matters of basic disagreement are in a

particular Community, they need to be talked out by the whole group, and in any decision made, respect for a variance of opinion must exist. The result of not dealing openly with such matters is a rising threshold of emotions that finally must break out in bitter and even destructive conflict.

6. *Duties—Some Agreed System for Handling Chores.* One continual pressure point was the failure of the boys to put out the garbage, a duty the girls insisted did not belong to them. Fortunately Diane liked cooking, and after work she would come home and prepare the evening meal, Karen, in the early months, accepted responsibility for the housework because she was not employed, so that the living areas were kept clean and reasonably tidy. Periodically a day was devoted to housecleaning. When Karen left the Community for several weeks it was necessary to make alternate arrangements for the food supplies and the cleaning.

A system was devised that worked moderately well. But without Diane's willingness to cook and several other members' actions on the end of brooms and mops, the health of the Community and the cleanliness of the house might have deteriorated to an alarming degree. The boys' level of tolerance of disorder was much higher than the girls', so that a running debate continued about what was acceptable for decent living and what was not. One suspects that all Communities will face a similar problem.

7. *New Members.* As a group develops its own life it begins to become proud of its identity as a special circle of people. In fact, the very development of a sense of belonging involves just such a division between those

who belong and those who do not. The invisible relational bonds that bind the group together are not perceptible to new members who unwittingly transgress tacit and unexpressed understandings that may cause the others to react instantly.

One of the hardest tasks therefore is the assimilation of new members so that their contribution is accepted, on its own terms, and newcomers learn, for their part, to understand what is required of them now that they belong to the group. On two occasions the Community attempted to include new members. The first resisted the Community's demands as unreasonable, the second was hurt by the Community's decision not to admit him as a member because agreement could not be reached about increasing the Community's personnel. One experienced the Community's demands as tyrannical; the other, as rejection. It was a long time before Community members could accept their failure in this area, and even longer before they were free enough to see strangers not as a threat to their life but as a potential enrichment of the total experience.

8. *Symbolic Existence.* By symbolic existence is meant activities that focus the energies of the group and symbolize its meaning. The first unified act of the Community was its participation in the Moratorium demonstration in Washington. Traveling across country together, the group took to collecting forks from restaurants, which at suitable moments were held aloft with a shouted, "Fork." Later, one could discover a large banner in the kitchen upon which was stitched an oversized felt fork.

On many occasions the group was rallied around such

unifying symbols as the word "fork" or the word "berfunkling," beloved because it was an ingroup term which meant all the best things about being together. Ritual acts such as burning incense or beginning each meeting by sharing the evening meal were crucial elements in the growth of Community awareness. The power they released was considerable because members entered into their meaning in a similar way and understood as one man what they represented to the group. Where such occasions and activities can be encouraged, the chances of growth into new understanding is greatly enhanced.

9. *Skilled Help*. It seems wise to have access to skilled help. Since the Community was linked with the Lay Academy, it was able to make contact with resource people quickly when the need arose. For example, Graham's bout in the hospital, due to an overdose, resulted in calling in a worker with drug users immediately for advice as to what should be done.

The presence of two members of the group who had training in various skills of group life and communication techniques also was important. The Community might not have survived its first months if creative ways of handling conflict had not been employed. Diagnosis of the reasons for interpersonal conflict was often necessary, and without trained personnel the Community could have easily destroyed itself. Perhaps the most important factor is the capacity of a group to recognize that it has reached an impasse and in that situation its willingness to ask for help. The high failure rate of communal experiments suggests that without skilled help at critical times, group disintegration is the likely result.

10. *Reentry*. The Community at its best provided for

its members a support system that enabled them to come to terms with their personal inadequacies and encouraged their attempts to grow into stronger, more mature images of themselves. But the removal of that support system can be traumatic if no alternative exists. Much of the group's time during the last weeks was spent discussing what members would do when the Community ceased. That included deliberately focusing on the question of where they would get help and support in their new environment.

For some the problem was acute because they had nowhere to go, or more particularly no one with whom they could trust themselves and be free to share their fears. One of the boys was linked up with professional help, others were able to find a sympathetic group of people at a church near where they were to live. But responsible action included caring beyond the time of living together in an endeavor to seek out for each member an alternate support system. It is a fact of life that all good things must come to an end sometime. The future offers us a hope of better things to come if the trouble is taken to plan intelligently for that new beginning which is always ahead of us.

INSIDE THE COMMUNITY'S LIFE

It is important to remind ourselves, as Kenneth Keniston says, that "what our society lacks . . . is a vision of itself and of man that transcends technology." [1] Correspondingly the present youth generation is seeking a deeply personal vision of man's future and destiny. Young people are searching for the dimension of the

Personal so that a path may open up for them through the mechanical wilderness of modern society.

The Community for Urban Encounter was composed of young adults who, like many of their contemporaries, were searching for a view of man that transcended technological definitions.

Through living together in Community they were seeking a new perception of the genuinely human that they could embrace. Intermingled was an authentic concern for man in his social state and an intensely private need for personal self-integration that would free them to be positive agents for social change in the urban environment.

The description that follows attempts to make explicit the factors that influenced the course taken by the advisers of the group and outlines a model for Community learning that takes due account of these factors.

The Problem of Authority

One basic decision that was crucial for determining what subsequently occurred was the acknowledged right of the Community to be responsible for the ordering of its own life. The implications of this decision included the recognition that staff personnel were present in the group as fellow members, to help guide and share, to facilitate and to enable, but not to direct.

The reason for this basic decision centered on the problem of authority. What can a young person affirm as valid and binding upon himself in modern society? If the Community is any guide, not the values of the System or the ideas of success involved in the march of technological progress. Being human means being able to choose in the light of the values that matter most to you. That is an intimate, personal deciding which cannot be programmed. Authoritarian instructions directing you to do this or that violate personal dignity. When the telephone bill arrived on an IBM card with instructions: "Do not bend, staple, spindle, or mutilate," one of the boys had to be prevailed upon not to bend and staple the card as many times as he could manage. But it was a significant and characteristic response. Rejection of authority, viewed as impersonal external demands, was strong in the Community.

It was not difficult to discover why. They viewed themselves as able and free enough to determine their own destiny. It was a right they cherished, but from their standpoint much of adult society denied them that right. Each was striving for independence, to be his own man, free to live out the consequences of his own decisions. They were seeking to be responsible in the only terms that ultimately matter, by discovering what they could commit themselves to wholeheartedly. But it had to be their choice, their decision, their struggle, not the one thrust upon them from without. It found its expression in a firm refusal to be subjected to either a predetermined content or dogmatic formulations about any subject. In particular the group would not accept an imposed leadership, an imposed task, an imposed curriculum. One source of real concern, therefore, was to develop a recognition and acceptance of the demands of society that are valid and proper. That was the external facet of the authority problem.

As for the Community, if any venture was to gain the group's loyalty, it had to arise from the group's own decision-making. In this, members were consistent with their own developmental needs and the mood of the youth culture of which it was a part.

How then could genuine authority be understood? Each member, including the staff personnel, had to earn the right to speak. A place in the group was won only by responsible action and consistent involvement. Out of this involvement one could offer opinions and have the opinions respected. The basis of the Community's life was responsible participation. From this source the characteristics of the Community's life emerged.

The Characteristics of the Community's Life

1. *Democratic.* In using the word "democratic," one risks destroying in the telling what actually happened. "Berfunkling" was not making proper decisions, it was being real. Several attempts made by Graham to have regular voting procedures were greeted with great scorn. Only in the beginning, before we became "berfunklers," were decisions made by majority vote. Later the group made decisions concerning administrative concerns easily and quickly. Where a person's sense of integrity was at stake the matter was taken with the utmost seriousness. Often that meant long hours of working toward a consensus, even if the process involved mounting frustration. But the Community lived by its faith that if someone is real, he must be respected.

Any member unduly threatened by a decision of the group had the right to withdraw from the meeting or to reject the common mind. In such cases it was also understood that any dissenting member, having chosen that road, must live out the consequences.

In practice it rarely happened, because "berfunkling" also meant caring. It would be untrue to suggest that the situation was without ambiguity. It was not. Many times to reach any kind of decision was a triumph. To get action on that decision bordered on the miraculous. But the Community was not trying to be efficient, only responsibly human. The process of arriving at a decision and the way of responding to opposition were as important as the decision itself. Despite the pain involved, decisions where possible were fought through to a consensus.

2. *Self-directed.* As a consequence of this view of the personal nature of authority, the Community in its formal gatherings set its own course. Any tasks undertaken had their origins in the needs of the group. These were not simply introverted in nature. For example, considerable time was spent working with Diane on the problem of teaching in a ghetto school and seeking to understand the social conditions that give birth to slum conditions and poverty. Where appropriate, outside resources were gathered to help the group work on a problem it recognized as important, but for the most part the Community members provided the resource for handling their own concerns. Responsibility to each other was fostered under such conditions.

It meant often that sessions planned for a particular evening had to be abandoned in order to deal with a crisis that had suddenly arisen. Because of the frequency of such unexpected changes of direction it is difficult to imagine how a formal course of education could have been profitably employed. In the Community's own understanding, however, "being mature means making

your own decisions, and becoming a person involves living out the consequences of your actions with people who are free to tell you in a caring way why you botched the job." It may seem like stating the obvious to point out that the struggle to be an inner-directed man was at the heart of the Community's life; but in an other-directed society. where men easily take on tailor-made images of the Self, perhaps the revolt is not recognized for what it is—a full-throated rebel yell for the Personal.

3. *Process.* The third characteristic has already been implicitly mentioned, the priority of process over content. The constantly moving network of relationships within the Community, with its unsettling effects, was of more interest to Community members than any sequential ordering of subject matter could possibly have been.

Members were actively and immediately involved in events in the Community. That was the point of their existential commitment, and what happened there took priority over all else. It was more important to discuss why the landlord had failed to put in the second shower, which resulted in the consequent jam-up in the mornings, than, say, the theory associated with crisis situations. The events of their daily existence provided the locus where they were most intensely alive. So the questions tackled were those which rose out of their life together, what the tangle of relationships revealed about being alive, and how tensions could be either tackled or avoided.

The counterpoint between what has authority and what is personal emerges as before. Again, in their concern for process, the members were revealing how closely they shared with their contemporaries the effect of being children of the electronic age. The primary mode was one of feeling engagement in events, not detachment from them nor reflection upon the total pattern. Such a priority raises interesting questions about many of the presuppositions of present educational systems. For identity formation, being oneself and understanding that self are crucial needs of the young. It is met, not by a careful preparation of instructional material, but by helping the young to reflect upon the meaning of their experience.

4. *The Now.* As a corollary of the priority of process over content, the fourth characteristic was a concentration upon the present. Community members were not interested in being "trained" for some conceivable future in which they might blossom to maturity. What they wanted to know had to be relevant to the present. No body of knowledge, no set of ethical principles, would suffice to assuage the thirst for meaning and interpretation of what was unfolding before their eyes.

No matter how interesting a discussion might be, it was often interrupted by someone who had observed another member withdraw inwardly from the conversation. Why doesn't this interest you? Doesn't it concern you that these things exist? It was not so important to resolve a discussion tidily as to confront and recognize where each person was in the discussion. Where are you? was the concern, and those who had most trouble in the Community were those who were frightened, lost, or confused in the presence of that concern. Where are you? Not sometime, not tomorrow, but now, in this energy-charged moment of drawing breath together.

It is this concern for the personal present which may help explain the current youth generation's refusal to buy packaged answers, which have been employed in the past. Only the questions seem to have enduring fascination. It is important to listen to one of the Community members, therefore, when he testified that the Community had taught him how to handle ambiguity, "to live with it and even to thank God for it." Because if you are convinced in principle that no one has the answers, you need to be able to survive, and, more, to learn to live joyously in a world of change. In any case, there is not time enough to spend working out solutions for questions that will no longer seem relevant when the answers are found. The future is now.

Factors Operative in the Group

1. *The Past.* Paradoxically, when viewed against the preoccupation with present concerns already mentioned, the past experience of the individual was a factor of major importance in determining his behavior in the group. Each member of the Community brought to the experience a vast residue of recollections, unfinished business, hurts, and needs from the past. With some, their relationships with their parents were still a source of distress. Others were fleeing from unhappy encounters with friends or lovers. In a few, there was a tired recognition that all the future could offer was a sad repetition of what had occurred in the past. But whether it was in the form of escape from the past or a joyous setting out for the next adventure that life might bring, each member carried with him luggage from previous experiences. In most, the past still appeared in the guise of a ques-

tion, Who am I? Repeatedly the past had to be dealt with before a creative future could become a real possibility.

One of the boys illustrates this point well. To be called a "good guy" seemed to raise him to a state of anger that was one step short of violent action. It was several months before the Community understood that the term had been applied to his father, now dead, who had failed to help his son at a crucial stage in his life. The "good guy" to his son, who had loved his father greatly, was someone who didn't fight for those he loved. The phrase was a negative symbol to him. Later he could handle the term with a rueful grin when it was applied to him, but before that stage was reached the Community went through many moments of genuine bewilderment trying to understand his angry reaction that appeared to be triggered off by a term generally regarded as a common place pleasantry.

2. *Developmental Tasks.* The average age of the group was approximately twenty-one. At the beginning of the year in the community none of the members were engaged to be married, though all were keenly interested in the topic. In one group exercise, Community members revealed that, next to a question about vocation, the demands of establishing intimacy with at least one other person most troubled them. If one uses Erik Erikson as a guide here, then this need to establish intimacy with another is one of the developmental tasks of the age group in question.

Caution should be exercised here, however, as the group displayed surprising variation. For some the struggle for independence was still going on. Others had small ego strength and were trying to fit together a self with which they were comfortable. Almost all were attempting to fashion a world view that would sustain them on the difficult journey they saw ahead.

But the life-stage of the group was a dependent variable that gave some interpretative framework with which to approach the meetings. If the crucial questions the group was asking could be isolated, then all was not darkness.

3. *The Youth Culture.* A third factor related to the place of the Community within the wider youth culture. The Community, speaking generally, was alienated by prevailing values and many of the prohibitions of society.

Perhaps the most startling divergence from young people of other times and other places was the clarity with which they saw the dehumanizing aspects of the society spelling out the horrifying, albeit sophisticated, tale of man's increasing inhumanity to man and his ravaging of the natural world.

They shared with their age group a burning sense of outrage that left them at once bewildered, frustrated, and angry. The heavy, impersonal weight of society's criminality, seemingly dedicated to destroying the most beautiful and precious values of mankind, bore down upon them.

Out of this cultural ethos their feeling of helpessness gave rise to the questions: What can I do? How can I live and act in this kind of society and keep my integrity? How can I save the things I cherish? They had a deeply held fear that for them there was no place where they could belong.

4. *The American Dream.* The final factor of consider-

able influence concerns the disintegrating influence of the American Myth. They experienced existentially Michael Harrington's insight voiced in *The Accidental Century* that "the present decadence is the corruption of a dream rather than a reality." [2] The American Dream appears to have lost its power to inspire the young, for it has turned out to be for them less a dream than a nightmare. As one of their contemporaries wrote: "I'm 22 years old and I'm tired. America has worn me out. I don't believe in God and I don't believe that America is the golden center of the Universe. You can get away with not believing in one of these, but not both." [3]

The question, What is the meaning of it all? plagued them. In terms cherished by Kevin: "What the hell! How much do we know?" With the loss of a supporting world view which assured them of the manifest destiny of the American nation, under God, the present youth generation is searching for a system of meanings that make sense of the whole farrago of events.

At heart this is a religious quest, but it is one shaped and formed by the culture in which it occurs. When the foundations are shaking, even the most deeply held convictions are called seriously into question. Such appears to be one of the prevailing moods of the young in American society today. It was shared in full measure by members of the Community for Urban Encounter.

In answering the questions about the characteristics of the Community's life-style and the variable factors working on and operating within the group, some description has been given of the situation from which productive new possibilities had to be extracted. It was clearly imperative that any steps taken to facilitate the group had to be congruent with the demands of the situation. Anything less would have meant disaster to the project. Thus it is important in any communal adventure to seek to discern the dynamics of the situation in order to use them productively. They can become the foundations upon which the Community's life is based just as surely as they can be the cause of its destruction.

EDUCATIONAL CONSIDERATIONS

There seems to be a growing awareness among some educators that the process of learning has to be freed from a servile bondage to content. What was intended in the project, educationally speaking, is contained in some words of Carl Rogers.

> The goal of education, if we are to survive, is the facilitation of change and learning. The only man who is educated is the man who has learned to learn: the man who has learned how to adapt to change: the man who has realized no knowledge is secure, that only the process of seeking knowledge gives basis for security. Changingness, a reliance on process rather than upon static knowledge is the only thing that makes sense as a goal for education in the modern world.[4]

Margaret Mead agrees substantially with Rogers that the task is to teach the young how to learn. "We must create new models for adults, who can teach their children not what to learn, but how to learn, and not what they should be committed to, but the value of commitment."[5] Value orientation is a crucial part of personal commitment.

The conviction that the real task was to facilitate change and learning in the Community provided two guiding principles in the education dimension of the Community's life. These two principles, Interaction and Continuity, were considered by Dewey to be fundamental to experiential learning.[6]

First, *interaction* between the external and internal dimensions of experience, according to Dewey, is the situation out of which the person grows. In the Community, if growth and change were to take place, involvement in the purposes and hopes of other people was unavoidable. There needed to be a concerted effort to interact creatively and purposefully so that members could grow to affirm and seek common goals together. When communication between members of the group was severed, any chance of group progress was lessened. It seems self-evident that the group progresses only as fast as the weakest members. So the freedom and capacity of members to relate to each other was a crucial element.

Flowing from this principle was a concern to enable the group to reflect upon the educative value of the experience of living together. Under its own momentum the group had decided to use its own life as resource for learning. The members had also given priority to process so that the raw data which they had at their disposal was generated out of the group itself. Therefore to interpret the significance of our common experiencing was the first guiding principle.

The second principle involved a *continuity* of experience that was of a positive and encouraging kind. A growing sensitivity to others' needs, when they arose in the house, enabled Community members to assist each other to learn from unhappy experiences and to foster creative moments that drew the Community together in a concern, affirming fellowship.

The intention was to facilitate in Community members the ability to learn from future experiences. The person who has learned to learn, as Dewey argued, is a person who can derive full meaning from his experience as it happens and culture this meaning into an integrated continuity of previous experiences, as well as to project new and exciting possibilities into the future.[7] He is a man who goes on learning because he is able to assimilate new ideas as they arise and integrate them into new ways of acting and responding.

The regular gatherings, held twice a week, were the occasions for reflecting upon events, a time for inquiry and searching, an opportunity to build more decisively on that foundation of trust which past experiences of living together had provided.

Without such regular meetings, the chance to deepen the sense of Community was not normally present, or, if present, seldom taken advantage of by members of the group. But because the Community shared the same physical environment, interaction and continuity of experience were always present as elements in the learning process.

In the formal meetings of the Community, therefore, it was possible to discover three steps supporting the group's struggles for understanding:

1. Recollection occurred of instances, events, feelings, or thoughts that had taken place and seemed significant.

2. An attempt was then made to discern why it "felt"

or "appeared" significant in order to grasp the reality present in the experience.

3. The final process was one of interpreting the events, and placing them in a framework of meaning that provided security for further growth and change.

A monthly Diary record of events was produced so that the key moments of the past month were recalled at the end of each month. The three steps outlined above cultured the meanings of these events into more informed perceptions of what had taken place.

The Diary Record, Therefore, Served Two Functions:

1. It served as a research instrument of major importance, because it preserved many of the significant moments when the symbolic and deeply personal levels of the Community's life were manifest. In retrospect, many Community members were able to articulate in a fresh way the meaning for them of the events described and what they had learned.

2. It functioned also as a learning tool which forced members to a deeper level of their shared experience. Members developed the capacity to reflect upon their own actions inside and outside the group. Thus the developing progress of the group was reviewed, and the Community was present at, and author of, its own growing maturity of life.

The presupposition of the whole enterprise was "Community" which provided the context of this learning experience. "Education," as Kurt Lewin wrote, "depends on the real state and character of the social group in which it occurs." [8] The social climate in the Community was just as crucial to the growth of its members as the air that Community members breathed. The idea of Community and what it grew increasingly to mean was the very concept upon which group members stood as they sought new understanding and fresh vision.

Which Educational Model Was Most Appropriate?

1. *The Action-Reflection Model and Its Failure.* It is worth reflecting first upon a model for learning that the group initially affirmed, but that proved inadequate, to illustrate how an educational design may inhibit rather than facilitate learning.

The program began with the expressed aim of encountering the city. So from the beginning an Action-Reflection Model seemed the most creative way of achieving this goal. It was expected that Community members would become intensely involved in some attempt at urban renewal from which they would return to the group to share problems, develop strategies, and reflect upon the significance of their undertaking.

But this design resulted in a fragmentation of the group because it was not possible to get all members to become engaged in some problematic situation in the city, or to get the Community as a single body to accept one particular project acceptable to all. It also served the function of directing attention away from the personal needs of the individuals in the Community. Experiences outside the group became the basis of the group's life, not the experiences of the group itself which all shared, to some degree, in common. The internal needs of Community members continually interrupted the flow of discussion concerning the city. Often, because no attention was paid to them, abrasive relationships between in-

dividuals flared up in a disguised form over an interpretation of what was happening in the urban scene.

It was also necessary to plan sessions in advance so
that each person could have equal time, thus inhibiting
spontaneity. The total effect was to cut against the grain
of the characteristics we have already discussed; it raised
authority questions, furnished an agenda other than the
Community's own, gave priority to "content" rather than
"process," and placed restriction upon the immediate demands of the Now. For reasons such as these the Action-
Reflection Model was abandoned as unworkable.

Another dimension involved here that needs comment
is that the "variables" had their influence also. Personal
and developmental needs, as representing intense internal pressures, were of more immediate concern than
social or ideological matters that were external to the
existential crisis of the individuals involved.

2. *The Basic Encounter Model.* By contrast, what
might be described as a "Basic Encounter Model," to use
Carl Rogers' term, was able to answer the demands for
flexibility and at the same time create a climate for
learning and growth. Authority was shared by the group,
which focused at meeting times on the urgent matters
that the Community felt to be troubling its life. The
responsibility of each member was to participate simply
as himself or herself. To share the task of facilitating
each other and to quarry for the meaning of our shared
existence beneath the burden of daily experience was the
procedure that was followed.

There was no set design to meetings. Sometimes small
groups were used to increase participation. Often the
group exercised a therapy function for one of its mem-

bers. Problems external to the group were discussed
where they impinged upon a person's concern. When it
seemed to be necessary, attention was paid to communication problems, and various experiments in communication took place. To illustrate, one device used by the
group was to equip each member with a green and a red
card. A show of the green card signified approval; the
red card, disagreement with what was being said. It is
safe to say that no member who was talking nonsense
did so for any length of time when confronted by a bar-
rage of red signals. On the other hand, a person uncer-
tainly seeking a means to share a problem with the group
found a source of courage in the supportive green cards
which flashed around the circle.

In sensing the acceptance and support of the group,
many a member was led to an honest confession of his
internal struggles, sense of failure, or prescience of doom
as he looked at the future.

Out of such moments of transparency many were able
to reassess themselves and find a new awareness as the
Community fed back an equally honest but supportive
response.

The body of literature defining the characteristics of
Basic Encounter Groups is vast and widespread. It is
assumed unnecessary to detail more completely what
takes place in a group in a continuing relationship such
as has been described. The real concern is to underline
again that the model was used because it was appropriate to the situation. It was appropriate also to the intentions of the designers of the project to facilitate and
encourage learning in Community members.

It can safely be said that, both painfully and joyously,

Community members were enabled by the group to expand their horizons and grow in self-understanding and self-worth. The different modes of perception that resulted gave birth to a rediscovered appetite for "Community" in its fundamental form. Members were awakened to a passion for life and a sensitivity to its possibilities that they had not known before.

While an internal uncertainty about the goals of the Community prevailed, coupled with a personal lack of identity and centeredness of Community members, no other method of handling the situation seemed appropriate. Although the right of the Community to order its own destiny meant a slower, more painful growth to maturity, it also furnished what the Community seemed to need most urgently: time for self-examination, time for identity formation, time to know the exhilarating experience of loving and being loved in a warm, affectionate Community of one's peers.

The Leader's Role and the Church's Responsibility

Two final considerations remain: some guidelines for understanding the leader's role, and a call to the church to consider the possibilities of "Community" as an integral part of youth ministry.

The Role of the Advisers

The overall function of the staff members was to be supportive of the group's efforts to handle its own problems. The advisers participated as members of the group, just as open to questioning and attack as any other person. If "authority" is seen as a group responsibility, then staff personnel are free to participate as regular group members. They cannot dominate the group without the problem of authority becoming a considerable stumbling block.

It should not be inferred from this comment that the adviser is only a member of the group. The point is that any authority he has in the group is earned by his participation and concern for the functioning of the Community.

The presence of the adviser as a member of the group gives him access to its inner collective life. He is able to interpret dialogues that occur at symbolic levels so that the inner and deeply personal life of Community members is open to him in a unique and special way.

The function of participant gives him the opportunity also to be an observer of the group, able to interpret it from the inside and yet maintain a suitable distance, necessary if he is to guide the group in the direction already defined as important: namely, to enable the group to reflect upon the educative value of the experience of living together and to facilitate in the Community the ability to learn from future experiences.

WHAT ROLES WERE IMPORTANT
FOR THE STAFF TO FULFILL?

1. *Trust.* The first function was to create a climate of trust in the group so that members became free to risk themselves. The climate of trust springs from the adviser's own ability to trust the group to react responsibly and to expect, even when the evidence is to the contrary, that the Community will return to a creative mode of being.

Responsible actions by the staff members demonstrate a similar level of commitment to the project as other members. In the case of the Community for Urban Encounter, this meant being present at all gatherings, willing to participate, and, if necessary, prepared to call the group back to its task.

2. *Interpretation.* A second function performed by staff members was to interpret the significance of what was happening between individuals or within the group. If one accepts that all behavior has meaning, then it follows that an explanation of what is taking place often enables individuals to understand their actions in a fresh way. The result may include changed behavior patterns that, supported by the group, open up new possibilities of acting and being for the individual concerned.

By pointing to the significance of what is taking place, the leader helps the group seek its own interpretations, which, when checked out with the perceptions of those present, can deepen the group's sense of sharing and being engaged in significant events.

3. *Support.* The continuing responsibility to encourage the Community to grow into new areas of acceptance meant, for the adviser, a constant supportive role of each person in the group. Many in the first instance needed assurance before they could trust either themselves or others. A pattern of unvarying concern for the health of the group and a willingness to confront members with the truth about their participation needed always to be tempered by the supportive role.

From experience with the group it seems clear that most people will not change their familiar methods of relating to others if they feel threatened by the group or members of the group. They are likely to change, however, when offered a stronger image of themselves. It is the acceptance and support of others that provides courage to try new ways of response. The adviser plays an important role in developing a supportive intentionality in the group.

4. *Integrity.* Most important, the staff can provide an integrity of personhood against which the group can test itself. Consciously assumed roles are in the long run secondary to a person's own style of existence. In representing to the group a constant level of participation, commitment, and responsible concern, an adviser can offer a viable way of being in the world.

The most powerful communication between adviser and group is at this indirect level. If the adviser has an undoubted personal integrity, and if the group understands that, no matter what happens, he will go on regarding them as persons who are worth time and effort, then much of what happens in the group can be diverted into creative channels.

The obverse of this observation is that the adviser must always speak to data that has arisen in the Community so that members are able to see on what basis observations are made. The comments and observations of the staff member must always be open to the Community's own perceptions, in order to prevent the leader's contributions from becoming dogmatic, critical, and tyrannical.

The Church and the Church's Responsibility

The ebb and flow of the present social scene throws up a considerable number of young people who have dropped out of college or become disoriented in their search for a realistic and meaningful life. A deep need for sympathetic understanding causes them to seek out a community of their peers in which they will be free from the judgments of adult society and free also to seek for a mature self-awareness.

The demands of communal living place considerable strain on individuals who have never learned to adapt to the needs of others. It brings them up hard against the inescapable realities of life. Rhetoric culled from the youth scene or fantasies nurtured in private dreams will not protect them against irregularities of conduct and inconsistencies of behavior.

Members learn that they are expected to act responsibly, not by unloving adults but by their peers. And the expectation includes not just a common commitment to "Community" but a common *level* of commitment, and a shared recognition of the rights and needs of all members of the Community.

Because of the large number of disenchanted young people, the church in fostering Communities such as the Community for Urban Encounter can provide an opportunity for young people, lost in the bewildering uncertainties of their generation, to find themselves in an environment they recognize as unchallengeably affirming of their struggle for meaning and purpose.

It offers the chance to many young people to learn how to relate to others, not as children to parents but as adults to adults. The experience of life in a community of one's peers forces a person to act responsibly and to grow into maturity.

Theologically speaking, the church has an unavoidable

responsibility to serve such young people for their own sake, in virtue of their need as human beings. When the church shows itself willing to risk personnel and money on projects that have no guaranteed return, its image begins to undergo a change in the minds of the young. At present, for the young people we are discussing, the church is a negative value to be lumped together with the government, the universities, the military. That the inner reality of the church is different from its public persona is a revelation of considerable impact to many young people.

Within the communal experience words and symbols emerge that reveal that the inescapable encounter with reality in the communal setting is fundamentally a religious one. Calvin wrote long ago that a change in one's self-concept could be correlated with a change in one's God-concept; the two are inextricably intertwined.

So the attempt to establish an integrated personality opens up all those questions of meaning and value which the church recognizes as based on genuine hunger for some ultimate Reality. It is to these existential questions that the good news of the gospel can be brought.

Although the words commonly used in discussion in the Community are far removed from the more self-consciously pious ones commonly used in church circles, they point to the same reality that lies behind words such as sin, repentance, reconciliation, and redemption. The reality is the same, the words are not.

But in the experience of the Community, where there was darkness, light came; where bondage, freedom; where death of self and all hope, resurrection and life. If one in faith seeks God's action in the midst of life, then there are signs that Christ, in Bonhoeffer's phrase, "takes form in a band of men."

Most of what the church represents theologically is present existentially in "Community." The need for forgiveness, the practice of service, the moments of genuine worship and celebration, the recognition that to save one's life is the same thing as to lose it: all these are present. God is constantly calling the church to new ways of responding to the needs of man. The model of communal living for the disenchanted young is surely one of them.

The real test of the church's willingness to give according to the need expressed will be whether it can forbear to ask the traditional question in the traditional way: "Were any saved?" Is there any way in which this question can receive any but an ambiguous response at the best of times?

But the distinction between long-term and short-term consequences of communal life can be drawn. It is unlikely that at this point in time the full significance of the year in "Community" will dawn upon the members of the Community for Urban Encounter. Only after some distance has been opened up will the full implications make themselves felt. Perhaps then, by way of response to the love that first grasped them, Community members will become in their turn concerned for the needs of their brothers.

QUESTIONS AND CONCLUSIONS

Some questions remain. Could the Action-Reflection Model implicit in the name Community for Urban Encounter have worked if more pressure had been brought to bear? For this particular Community, the answer seems to be a decided No. One suspects that despite the infinite variations, styles, and intentions of particular Communities, it will always be difficult, given the variables outlined for a community of young people, to be consistently faithful to an Action-Reflection Model of learning.

Will the members of the Community now be free, without its support, to act responsibly? No decisive answer is possible except to record the conviction that for some the year was as important a step in the direction of being free as any they have taken in their lives.

In the life of the Community for Urban Encounter, the Basic Encounter Model proved to be a valuable guide for the venture, able to cover the circumstances, flexible enough to assimilate new twists of direction, and sufficiently free from problems of authority to encourage freedom of growth in those who participated.

Perhaps the only certainty one has in working with young people is, as Theodore Roszak says, that "Youth Culture is grounded in an intensive examination of the Self, of the buried wealth of personal consciousness." [9] *That being so, the goal to facilitate the search for oneself, the fostering of the capacity to learn from experience how to learn, seems the only live option before those who work with the young in Community.*

The church should be involved in this frontier where the need obviously exists. In addition, the search for personal vision in the quest for Community reminds us again that we cannot be human alone. A deep personal sense of "Community," of belonging and caring and giving, is what the church exists to symbolize as possible among men through Jesus Christ.

Paradoxically, as we attempt to enter into the fullness of that experience, the young may serve as our teachers.

NOTES

1. Kenneth Keniston, *The Uncommitted* (Delta Books, Dell Publishing Company, 1963), p. 423.
2. Michael Harrington, *The Accidental Century* (Harmondsworth: Penguin Books, Ltd., 1968), p. 9.
3. Anonymous, in *Time* magazine.
4. Carl Rogers, *Freedom to Learn* (Charles E. Merrill Books, Inc., 1969), p. 104.
5. Margaret Mead, "Youth Revolt: The Future Is Now," *Saturday Review,* Jan. 10, 1970, p. 113.
6. John Dewey, *Experience and Education* (William Collins Sons & Co., Ltd., 1967), Chs. 1 and 2.
7. *Ibid.*
8. Kurt Lewin, *Resolving Social Conflicts* (Harper & Brothers, 1948), p. 3.
9. Theodore Roszak, *The Making of a Counter Culture* (Anchor Books, Doubleday & Company, Inc., 1969), p. 62.